Red on Gold

NAM PHUONG

Red on Gold

The true story of one woman's courage and
will to survive in war-torn Vietnam

AN ALBATROSS BOOK

© Nam Phuong 1991

Published in Australia and New Zealand by
Albatross Books Pty Ltd
PO Box 320, Sutherland
NSW 2232, Australia
in the United States of America by
Albatross Books
PO Box 131, Claremont
CA 91711, USA
and in the United Kingdom by
Lion Publishing plc
Peter's Way, Sandy Lane West,
Littlemore, Oxford OX4 5HG, England

First edition 1991

National Library of Australia
Cataloguing-in-Publication data

Nam Phuong
Red on Gold

ISBN 0 86760 138 8 (Albatross)
ISBN 0 7459 2187 6 (Lion)

1. Nam Phuong
2. Vietnamese – Australia – Biography
3. Vietnam – Politics and government –
   1945–1975
4. Vietnam – Politics and government –
   1975–   I. Title

920.72

Printed and bound by The Book Printer, Victoria

Contents

To my parents,
for their love for me and
for the faith they had in me;
*to my sisters, my brothers
and their families,*
with my regrets for not
being able to share with them
the freedom I have found;
to my husband,
for bringing such joy into my life
and helping me complete this book.

Foreword

This is the story of the indomitable human spirit, the spirit which could ride out courageously the ferocious clash of differing ideologies within a country. This portrayal of the hardships and anguishes of an extended family encapsulates the very real story of Vietnam. It is a cry from the heart of an extremely brave Vietnamese woman, who brings the reader even closer to the truth of the conflict of her native country.

As an indigenous Australian, I am able to relate somewhat to the 'conquered' feeling experienced by the writer and her family. My forebears also knew dispossession and forced adaptation. Like the brave Nam and her fellow Vietnamese who have arrived on our shores, the Australian Aborigines feel our land is a haven, but the process of adapting long and difficult.

This is a book that tears at the heart, but the spirit shines through like God's radiant light. I sincerely recommend the reading of *Red on Gold*.

Neville T. Bonner, AO

7

'Oi! Neu toi khong tin chac rang se thay on Duc Gie Ho Va tai dat ke song, thi toi han da nga long roi.'

Thi thien 27: 13

'I would have despaired unless I had believed that I would see the goodness of the Lord in the land of the living.'

Psalm 27: 13

1

Mekong delta disaster

I SAT WITH MY BACK flat against a tall tree in the midst of the jungle, exhausted. My face felt on fire. My back was as stiff as wood. I was slowly recovering from the painful discomfort of not being able to relieve myself. On the ground opposite me was Khoa, my thirteen-year-old nephew. He lay on a large sheet of nylon, an old military parachute, trying to rest after the harshest day of his life. He needed a good bath and clean clothes, but we had more important matters to worry about.

After travelling all day along the river from My Tho, a provincial town about fifty kilometres south-west of Saigon, we had finally reached this swampy island, our secret escape rendezvous. During the long hours on a small motor boat, we were not allowed to talk or even move about. There was a constant fear of being recognised by the river security police. To add to our discomfort, the bright hot sun followed us relentlessly all day.

From the moment my nephew Khoa and I were led to this secret spot of wild trees, thorn bushes and giant weeds surrounded by water, half fresh and half salty, I had thought I was in the valley of death. An eerie silence engulfed us. I tried hard not to be afraid. I needed to think clearly to deal with the dangers around me and protect my small nephew. But the shock had made me immobile, as if dead.

Louis, a Vietnamese reflecting his French influence in his name, was my contact for the escape. He threw a blanket-sized bundle on the ground near me and sat on it. Next to him was his girlfriend.

'The "big fish" is coming tonight!' Louis said, sighing with relief.

I glanced at him inquisitively. 'Are you sure we're leaving tonight?'

'Why not?' He stared at me, surprised that I asked. 'The escape is today. That's why I brought you here as I promised. Don't you believe it?'

'Yes, I do! But you never know for sure about this sort of thing,' I answered defensively.

Louis' girlfriend turned to me. 'Oh no, don't say that! Think positively and everything will be good!'

I felt all my strength and hope for a safe departure built up over many months disappear instantly with this reliance on superstition.

'Where are my brother and my other auntie?' my nephew suddenly sat up and asked. He gazed around the area in vain. His voice was unsteady. 'I thought I would see them here.'

'Oh no! They're at another spot around here with another group of people. Don't worry! You'll see them soon,' Louis said to calm him down.

Louis looked at his watch and again stated firmly, 'It's tonight, for sure! I've seen the big fish. It's well equipped with all the instruments for sea, fuel and plenty of food!'

'Where are we at the moment, Louis?'

Louis did not answer me. But I thought, why should I worry about this? If I'm leaving tonight then nothing else matters to me.

'I'm going for a swim now! Let's have a quiet swim and enjoy the water before saying goodbye to all the troubles of this life here.' So saying, Louis stood up, helped his girlfriend up and both ran towards the river like two little children.

The afternoon sun's rays penetrated the thick foliage into the heart of the jungle, like a cluster of lights from an enormous torch. I felt fearful, thinking of the darkness which would soon surround me.

'Auntie, I feel itchy all over my arms and legs!' grumbled Khoa, half asleep. He scratched his bare arms and legs. 'Ah, mosquitoes! Look, Auntie!'

Following his finger, I saw thousands of mosquitoes buzzing noisily in and out of the foliage around us. Panicking, I screamed into my nephew's ears. 'Be quick, dear! Help me put up the mosquito net!' I opened a large straw bag at the base of a tree nearby. 'What's the matter?' I asked myself. It was not my bag! It was Louis'! I looked around. There must be another bag made of straw the same as this one.

I was shocked to think that Louis had taken my bag purposely. An escape from the escapees! However, I had to find the mosquito net first. I dug right to the bottom of this bag and, as I guessed, a mosquito net was there. I pulled it out and stood up. After ten minutes' searching, my nephew and I found something strong enough to suspend the net from and we sat under it, safe from the mosquitoes, talking and waiting for Louis and his girlfriend.

'Auntie, this isn't our mosquito net, is it?'

Khoa's question brought back a sickening feeling. 'But where are they now? And what is the explanation about the missing bag?' I thought.

'No, it's not ours. I took it from Louis' bag,' I replied.

'Why? Where's our bag?' Khoa asked, raising his voice.

'Our bag is not here!' Khoa looked around to make sure I was right.

'I have a sick feeling that there is no big fish at all! Nothing's going to happen tonight. Louis and his girlfriend have left us,' I admitted with reluctance.

'You mean that's why they took our bag and left theirs here to . . .?' Khoa hesitated to finish.

'Yes, to confuse us! That's how I feel!'

I had thought Louis was a trustworthy friend — I did not want to think wrongly of him! But Louis still had not come back. I looked at my small nephew. I felt helpless! If he asked what I would do to rescue us from this crisis, I would have to say, 'I don't know! I really don't know!'

The sun dropped below the horizon. The gloom deepened.

'Auntie, it's my brother! It's him!' Khoa burst into a cheer when the side of the mosquito net was suddenly pulled up and my older nephew appeared inside.

'Is it you, Lam? Oh, thank God!' In the dying twilight under the mosquito net, I grasped the hands of my sixteen-year-old nephew as a kind of support.

'Where were you, brother?' Khoa anxiously asked. 'How did you know we were here?'

Lam seemed surprised. He said, 'Didn't Louis tell you, Auntie? He came around to our spot and let us know that both of you are here. Louis wanted me to come here to take you both to our group.'

'But why did he have to ask you to come over here? We thought he would come back after his swim and would take us over to meet you!'

Lam did not say a word. He was always a quiet one. He thought of what Louis had whispered to him: 'Don't leave them alone! I have to swim across the river to check the hidden fuel which has been concealed under the water, ready for tonight.'

We were all quiet. We felt we had no alternative but to think our friend had cheated us.

'Auntie, can we pray now?' Lam asked.

'Yes, dear,' I answered my older nephew with no hesitation; but I thought, 'How do we pray? Do we pray for a miracle for tonight that we will leave Vietnam safely? Or do we pray for a safe return to our home in Saigon?'

I felt confused. My present situation made me feel God was too far away from me — I was just an earthly thing whom he would not have time to listen to. Or had what I was doing been against his plan for me and so he would not help me now? I wished I could understand these things more clearly.

We became conscious of a cold wetness under us, even though we sat on the sheet of nylon under the mosquito net. It was certainly not rain from outside. Hurriedly we pulled up the net and touched the ground. Water was everywhere.

I had no idea whether this was a serious flood or an evening high tide. 'We might drown!' I thought. In the darkness we touched each other to make sure we were close together.

'Auntie, try to find your bag and your *non la*,' Lam whispered.

I groped in the dark for Louis' bag and my hat. The bag was on the root of a tree and still not wet! Lam grasped it from me and searched in it.

'Ah, wonderful! Incenses and matches! Auntie, we must beat the rising tide as soon as we can! My idea is that we'll all sit down close in a circle. I'll hold the incense sticks and you'll light the matches and burn the incense for me. At the same time, Khoa can hold the hat to cover what we'll be doing, to avoid the wind, but most importantly to avoid being seen by fishermen from the river.'

Lam continued. 'After that, we'll all bend. You'll be close behind me. Hold the *non la* over my side to the front, to cover the burning incense for me. Khoa will be close behind you. Then I'll guide you both to move on to the other group. I'm sure we can work out together how to get out of this jungle. Have you got the idea, Auntie?'

'Yes.'

The water was covering the area at an astounding rate. My older nephew bent down and swept the burning incense lightly across the damp surface, while moving himself forward along the walking track. My younger nephew and I followed him closely — the burning incense was only enough to light up a tiny area.

'If the water keeps coming up so quickly I won't be able to follow the track!' Lam whispered apprehensively.

I felt useless. I whispered to myself, 'Louis, why did you do this terrible thing to me?'

Our clothes were soaked with the cold water. But we kept moving in the darkness until we heard the boisterous sounds from the other group.

'Oh God! Help us to get home safely!' Tearfully, my sister, who had been with the other group, grasped our small nephew in her arms.

It was about two o'clock in the morning. A terrifying silence had settled on the whole jungle.

I was struggling along in the darkness, stumbling blindly in muddy water full of weeds and thorns. My feet and legs hurt as they hit unseen objects. We were fighting for a way out to the edge of the water. I grasped hold of a bit of the shirt of the leading man, to make sure I did not lose track of him. Behind me were my small nephew, my sister and my older nephew. The rest of the people who were following the leading man were a young woman and about ten young men.

After a flurry of frenzied arguments about whether we should leave the place immediately for our safety, or stay to wait for the big boat which would hopefully come sooner or later tonight, we finally divided into two groups. Vu, a man in his late thirties, volunteered to lead the people who wished to go home immediately. The other group, including young men in their early twenties, chose to stay.

I suddenly had a feeling that my older nephew was not behind us. Panicking, I pressed my small nephew's hand and whispered, 'Where's your brother?'

'He must be behind among the others!' Khoa answered.

After quietly checking with people behind, I realised that he was not with us any more. He had gone back to the other group without telling us. 'Should we walk back to find him?' I whispered to my sister. 'I don't want to go home without him!'

Vu's startled voice from the front brought to a sudden end any thought of turning back. 'Oh my God! We're so far away from the mainland!'

The pale moonlight from the east revealed an immense area of water. It was an estuary of the Mekong River system leading to the South China Sea.

'To get across to the mainland, we desperately need a boat from an early worker of some sort! I don't think it's possible to hide our identity and reason for being here,' Vu said. 'Does everybody agree to tell the truth — that we're *vuot bien* people (those who cross the international border illegally)?'

There was no sound from the abandoned people sitting in the dark. But everybody, aware of their hopeless situation, knew they had no alternative. I thought to myself, 'I've got to go home! It's strange to think I might be arrested and be a prisoner!'

'Hello there! Would you please stop for a moment?' Vu took the risk, shouting across the river the moment he heard the sound of an oar stirring the water.

'Who are you? Where are you?' a male voice shouted across the river, breaking the serene silence of the early morning.

'I need your help! I'm near the biggest bush hanging over the water!'

I felt fear! We were now in this unknown man's hands. Would he be kind? Would he help us, or be untrustworthy? Perhaps he was an angry *cong an*, the security marines, hunting the country's traitors!

Vu pushed us three women to the front to prove that we weren't dangerous.

'My goodness! How many are there altogether?' the man cried out as he saw us move close to the water. He was all dark with a wide-brimmed hat, standing shakily against the gloomy moonlight at the end of his large sampan. 'No, no! Too dangerous! I can't do anything for you!' The man shook his head constantly.

'Hang on! Please kindly listen to me! We need your help! Please help us to cross the river to the mainland. That's all we ask for!' Vu anxiously insisted.

'What the hell are you doing here in this jungle?'

The man seemed to have softened his voice while he tried to secure his sampan by grabbing a weedy bush. The tiny spark glowing from his cigarette was not enough to reveal his face.

'Please pity us! We're harmless! We tried to escape, but we were cheated! They abandoned us!' Vu lowered his voice miserably.

'Well!' The man said slowly. 'I will miss a most valuable load of charcoal if I stay here and help you!'

I could not judge by his voice if he was an honest person; but Vu was determined not to let him go. He pleaded with us in the dark. 'Everybody be ready to give him any possessions you have! Okay? We can't afford to get stuck here until dawn! I must keep my cash for our bus tickets!'

Then he turned back to the river. 'We'll be fair to you for sure, my friend!'

Within a minute some valuable watches and gold rings were handed to the man. At the same time we tried to climb down to the sampan as quickly as we could.

Finally we all settled into the sampan. For a while we all sat quietly. Each pursued a different thought. The sound of the oar stirred up the water roughly as if the sampan was about to sink. It felt very unstable. I thought of Lam, my older nephew, and my heart ached. Only a few hours earlier he had been my support and security; now he was alone and his situation critical. I prayed silently for his safety. I thought of my parents. They were probably waiting to hear the good news of our escape, even though they had never wanted to be separated from any of us.

The sampan suddenly lurched heavily on a huge damp surface near the river bank, forcing us all back to reality. 'You have to wade through the mud to the bank! Sorry, that's the problem in this area!'

Without delay, the man pushed his boat back to the deep water and rowed away. A huge muddy bank, black and stinking, extended about fifteen metres from where we were to the dry mainland.

'It's only four o'clock!' The sampan man suddenly yelled back to us. 'The first bus is at five. You can wait at the eating shop over there!'

From the distance we could see a small light twinkling

in the murky morning.

The mud was up to our waist; it took all our effort to pull ourselves through the muck. With each step we became more desperate to reach the bank. 'Excuse me! Will you be kind enough to give us some water to wash the mud off?'

Several people were busy preparing breakfast and coffee in their shop to sell to local working people who started early. An old woman stared at us then said, 'Come on! To the back!'

Quickly she showed us to the back of the kitchen.

'*Vuot bien*, eh?' She groaned. 'Silly, absolutely silly! Be quick and get rid of the mud; otherwise you will be caught! Here's some water!'

All that had happened to me since yesterday was like a nightmare! The strain of possibly being arrested was so great that I was unaware of what had been going on around me until the bus driver urged all the passengers to get off for a police check at the ferry.

'Hey woman, your travel permit?' the local police officer asked a passenger angrily.

'Oh dear! We don't have a travel permit!' I whispered in fear to my sister.

'None of us have!' my sister answered. 'I think we have to make up a reason as if this is a one-day trading trip!'

But our faces were unfamiliar to the local people and our odd attitudes revealed our secret. We stood separately from the crowd at the ferry and gave an unconvincing reason for travelling without a permit.

'Shut up and follow us! We know very well who you are!' The two police pushed us roughly towards a three-wheel taxi which had just passed by and ordered the driver to transport us to the local police station.

* * *

After three days being detained at the local temporary prison where we had all been arrested first, we were transferred to the larger central prison.

As soon as I appeared for the second day in the interrogation room with the guard who escorted me from a solitary confinement cell, the police officer jumped into the same questions which I had been asked many times by the local police at the temporary prison.

'How much did you people pay for this escape?'

'Two teals (about $US 200 worth) of gold per person! But I didn't have gold. I sold all the goods I had at home to pay for this,' I said.

'Rubbish!' The northern policeman angrily shouted at me. 'Only two teals! If so, where's all the rest of your gold? Where do the Chinese in your group hide their gold?' He stopped for a moment, then softened his voice. 'If you tell me the truth, you'll be safe. Understand?'

The interrogator said those last words slowly as if he wanted to convey the idea that if I revealed where all the gold was I would be free and would not be transferred to the provincial prison.

I certainly did not know anything about the Chinese young people whom I had briefly met in the jungle. But actually I had observed one truth. After only a few days in the jungle, I had sensed how dishonest people are.

'I'm sorry,' I replied. 'I don't know.'

'Your father is a church minister, is he?' asked the interrogator, continuing to give me a cold, stern look. I glanced at him to try to sense his real thoughts about me. Nothing was revealed.

'Yes, he is,' I said.

The northern security officer, in his crumpled, baggy khaki uniform and the black *dep rau*, the legendary sandals made out of truck tyres which Ho Chi Minh and his soldiers used to wear in the jungle, looked coarse. He bent down to his bare wooden table and wrote something on the stack of crumpled dirty sheets that passed for a note pad with a ballpoint smudged with runny blue ink. He cleared his throat roughly, stood up, then spat into the corner of the room. For a moment I could not stop thinking bitterly, 'How can I comply with the orders of such an uncultivated figure of authority?'

'Do you know Do Huy Lam at all?'

'Yes, he's my older nephew.' I felt faint after this answer. I thought, 'My God, Lam is arrested for sure. Otherwise the police would not have known his name.'

'Liar! Yesterday you said you didn't know anyone else in the party except your sister and that little boy with you!'

The whole world around me all of a sudden collapsed! The picture of my small nephew standing miserably in the courtyard and the trembling sound of my sister's voice tore at my heart.

'Helping your auntie carry food home from the market, that's all you have to say if the police ask you! Say no more! Can you remember that dear?' my sister had told our small nephew. But the police slapped him harshly when he said no more to them.

A fist rapped on the wooden table dragged me back to where I was at present.

'Are you a Christian?' the interrogator asked.

'Yes, I am,' I said apprehensively.

The police officer paused for a moment, then continued the interrogation. 'Why did you want to leave Vietnam? Tell me!'

'I'm jobless and have nothing to live on.'

I said this slowly and clearly to make him believe that this was the main reason. In fact, being jobless resulted from my being mistrusted by the communist liberation authorities. I had a long record of working in the past with foreigners, American and Australian. The company where I worked before the fall of Saigon had been under suspicion as an American CIA network. But I thought it would not be wise to point this out and so end up in prison or one of the so-called re-education camps to be brainwashed.

'I see! Did you pray before you joined this escape?' He stared at me with a cold look as if his challenging question to me would be far beyond my willingness to answer.

'Yes, I did.' I felt my head was burning and my face was stiff after that answer.

'You did!' The police officer stared at me mockingly; then he turned his face upward and blew a thick chain of smoke up into the air after drawing a deep breath from his cheap locally-made cigarette. 'But he didn't help you, did he?'

For the first time my real self and my faith were in confrontation with the views of my captors. I had never prepared myself for such a situation and felt weary and overwhelmed. I regretted what I had done. All I wished at that moment was to go back home, eat and sleep and never let this happen again!

The sharp voice of the interrogator again struck my ears. 'Can't you answer me? Did he answer your prayer? He didn't, did he?'

A stack of papers was all of a sudden thrown in front of me together with a cracked ballpoint. 'You must write your life story!'

The man drew a last whiff of smoke from his burning cigarette-end, threw it on the dusty floor, then angrily crushed it under the toe of his sandal and disappeared.

And I recalled my life.

2

Arrest in the night: 1945

THE DIM LIGHT FROM A NIGHT LAMP was scattered around the bedroom. I saw my father quietly pull up the side of the mosquito net to let himself out of bed. For a couple of seconds he seemed to listen for something; then cautiously he walked to the bedroom window. The night was silent. I could hear nothing except thousands of insects. Always after heavy rain at night they uttered their rhythmic sounds.

I felt a chill down my back. 'Papa, where are you going?' I murmured. Although I could not see him very well through the thick mosquito net I heard my father whisper, 'Be good and quiet, dear! I'll come back to you right away!'

I thought that a thief must be trying to break into our house — not that I had ever seen one! In my bed, like a live eel wrapped in a lotus leaf, I made no move at all until I heard a quiet knock at the front door. It sounded as though the door was being opened. I froze.

It must have been about five minutes since my father left his bed, but he had not yet come back. 'Papa, where are you?' I felt so scared being by myself. Tears began running down my cheeks as I called out to my mother from my bed. 'Mama, where's Papa?' I called.

My mother woke up. She was very tired and had been busy with the new baby during the night. In a sleepy husky voice she calmed me down as if she was worried that I was being difficult at night and would wake up the baby. 'But Mama, Papa's not here!' I sobbed.

My mother moved slowly from her bed. I heard the sound of her feet on the floor as she sought her thongs. She came close to me. 'What is it, dear?' she asked. I burst into tears, telling her what I had seen a few minutes ago.

'Don't cry, darling! I'll go and find him. Everything's all right!' Then my mother walked to the front room, leaving me wondering whether she knew where my father would be.

All was quiet. I started to count every minute from the time my mother left me. There was no sound at all. I imagined that the thief was being chased by my father. I felt paralysed with fear, not knowing how my mother would react if she actually saw the thief. I prayed silently that they would not be hurt.

Suddenly my mother appeared in the doorway and rushed to my bed. 'Papa had to go into town early. Don't worry, darling! He'll come back soon.' Then she carried me over to her bed and laid me down between her and the baby. Although still young, I sensed in my mother's voice that something terrible had happened to my father. I dared not say anything, but my fear for my father increased as every minute passed. I lay awake in bed until the first rays of the sun broke through the window.

Everything outside was wet and soaked with water after the heavy storm early the previous night. The bamboo front gate had collapsed and some banana trees in the backyard laden with fruit had been knocked down by the storm. On the left hand side of the front doorway, the thick jasmine bush was in tatters, its flowers scattered on the dirt.

My sisters and I felt very sad waking up in the morning without my father. My parents had a new baby, a fourth daughter. My father was wonderful. He looked after my sisters and me, allowing me in his bed at night and so freeing my mother to care for the new baby. This morning my mother looked worried and sad. As we sat down for breakfast, she asked us to pray for our father who, she said, 'is away from home'. I saw my mother arrange for a neighbour to help with the housework, especially to look after the baby for her. Then my mother got dressed and went away.

Later that day I learnt what had happened that night. After my father had gone out, my mother went to the front room and saw that the door was unlocked. She stood at the open door and looked into the darkness. She still did not see him. 'Darling, where are you?' she called into the dim moonlight. There was still no sign of my father. Suddenly she saw what appeared to be a tall dark figure moving towards her. 'No, it's not him!' my mother said to herself in disbelief. Then she saw eyes, white and big, piercing into hers. A soldier! Yes, a tall black French African soldier rushed at my mother.

'Shut up! Move inside the house or you'll be killed!' the soldier angrily ordered, pointing his gun at my mother's chest. She immediately drew herself inside the house and breathlessly walked back to the bedroom.

Although shocked by the event, my mother guessed what might have happened to my father. He had been arrested by the soldier when he innocently opened the front door. The African soldier must have been assigned by the French to watch my parents' house all night.

As evening fell, my mother returned home, tired and lonely. She had gone to town to visit a missionary to inform him what had happened to my father the previous night, hoping the missionary would be able to help find out where my father was, and what had actually happened to him.

Some friends who belonged to my father's church visited my mother and tried to comfort her, but could do nothing for her. Some went to the church which was next to our home to pray for my family.

This is what she found out. My father was being detained by the French at the local sûreté, or CID office, together with other people from our village who were arrested on the same night. All were suspected of being Viet minh, an anticolonial movement formed to fight against the French occupation of Vietnam. The French believed it was essential to search out and destroy this movement at its source.

Most of the French officials seemed to have respect for the missionaries and for their religious activities. My mother was right when she decided to share the news about my father with Mr Cadman, an American missionary. He contacted the central sûreté office and found out that my father had been held at the local security post for identity investigation. The missionary explained that my father was a clergyman, and requested my father's case be considered with that in mind. The immediate favourable response from the French captain, head of the security office, surprised even the missionary. Three days later my father was released!

About fifteen men from our village, including my father, were arrested that night. The soldiers had suddenly broken into their homes when all the families were in bed, woken them up, searched every corner of their houses then, without any explanation, had taken them to a truck and driven them to the local security post. My father's arrest had been a little different from the others; he had been inadvertently arrested when he just happened to check around the house after hearing some strange noises.

In the darkness, the soldier had seized my father, pointed his gun at him, twisted his hands behind his back, then pushed him from behind to a military truck parked around the corner. Everything happened so suddenly that my father did not realise what the situation was until he saw the truck.

The temporary prison was a row of several wooden cubicles in a large open area with a high thick barbed wire fence. Each was big enough for seven or eight people sitting flat on the dirt floor. Several guards with guns constantly walked around the outside. The captives were in a state of confusion, anxiously awaiting the next possibly fatal step from the security office. As a man who had devoted his life to his faith, my father did what he could by praying silently.

He had not thought my mother could do anything for him. He longed only to have a word with her before anything more tragic occurred. All the people in the cell were worried and confused. Suddenly my father was called to report himself to the chief of security at his office.

'Je suis le pasteur d'église évangélique.' My father thus introduced himself to the captain after he was escorted by a soldier to the office. The French captain looked at him from head to toe. Until that moment my father had not realised how messy he was; in dirty pyjamas and with feet bare, he appeared like an old rag. For three days the arrested people were given no chance at all to wash and clean themselves.

The captain, however, understood the situation. 'Bon jour, monsieur le pasteur.' In his military straightforward manner he stood up behind his desk, stretched out his right hand to shake my father's hand. The captain then expressed his regret at what his soldiers had done. He ordered a pair of clean clothes and shoes be brought for my father. The guard showed him to a small bathroom next to the office. There he cleaned himself up, got changed and was freed. In the oversized clothes and shoes, he looked like a clown at a children's play.

It was wonderful to have my father back home; but, despite the happy outcome, the frightening incident had a strong impact on my early childhood. From that time, the fear of losing my father, leaving my mother to struggle alone, dominated my thinking day and night, though I was too young to understand why life had to be like it was.

It was 1945, the Japanese had been conquered, and the French had re-established their colonial rule upon Vietnam. The Vietnamese people had survived by running to escape the furious bombing from the French against the Japanese. People had nothing other than their bare hands and feet to start life again; yet they now began a new ordeal — the constant fear of being mistaken by the French as Viet minh guerrillas or sympathisers. Places under suspicion were continually checked by the security forces in order to hunt down suspected Viet minh. Random checks were often made at night so that the guerrillas could not easily escape.

The darkness of night was the worst time. Men could never have a good night's sleep without worrying about suddenly being dragged out of their houses by the local police. Then — it depended on how large the random check was — up to a hundred men would be made to sit down on the ground somewhere along the road from midnight until late the next morning, waiting for the search of the whole area to be over. After that, each man had his personal identity checked. Some were lucky and were able to return home soon after that. Others for unknown reasons were suspected of being Viet minh; they were transported to another place for more serious investigation.

My small world as a little girl was constantly disrupted. Though it seemed his position in the church made my father a more trusted person to the French than some others, our home was still checked as often as the others. My father was at times taken out for a few hours for identity checking, then was returned home. At other times he was taken away for a day or a week. The same situation happened everywhere to most people my parents knew. We constantly prayed for my father's return when he was arrested and we believed in it.

When my father was away, I missed the close atmosphere in the evening. My sisters and I often gathered around my father's desk when he was busy working on his sermons, watching the flame burning from the rough clay lamp. The lamp was shaped like a champagne glass in which lard and a lamp-wick were used as fuel. Even when my father was concentrating on his work, he still wanted to be close to his children. To keep us busy next to him, he would give us a riddle — like this: 'Where does the flame go when you blow it away?' And this left us confused until my mother urged us to go to bed.

On other evenings when the moon was full, my eldest sister and I would go for a walk with my father along the winding path over the paddy fields. When it was close to harvest time, the bountiful rice turned to a brilliant golden colour; under the shining moonlight, it was like streaming golden hair.

But that peace was gone. Now we lived in an uncertain situation, and were worried most of the time. One evening, the police came to our house again and my father was once more taken away. He did not return until two months later. We were so shocked at his disappearance. During that time we prayed hard; tears mingled with our food at the table every day.

One day, to our great surprise, my father finally came back home. The tension and stress of the past weeks were apparent on his face; but he remained strong in his faith. My father was actually imprisoned this time without being questioned. Several times he was taken out of his cell with a group of about twenty men from other cells who he believed had been captured at the same time. They were made to sit down in line on the ground in the hot sun for hours without being told the reason. Several armed guards walked around watching them. At first my father thought it was a kind of punishment.

One morning, a group of French officials confronted the prisoners. The guards ordered all the prisoners to stand up with their hands behind their backs. My father was horrified when he saw a person appear quietly among the French, his head covered in a large unbleached linen sack, the kind of rough bag used for rice or flour. This kind of sack, called *bao bo* in Vietnamese, covers the man's head and has two small holes so he can see. My father recalled what he had heard from other people about this.

The French used a number of Vietnamese men who were unknown to the local people. They were collaborators. Hiding their face and the upper part of their body inside the sack, these people were supposed to tell the French who were the real Viet minh. In a day of *nhin mat*, 'recognising faces', if the collaborator stopped in front of a captive and nodded his head, the captive, rightly or wrongly, was often executed. Rumours about these dangerous men soon spread around the country. They were considered traitors.

My father stood there in horrible shock. The *bao bo* walked slowly up and down in silence; not a word was heard from the officials or the guards. Suddenly he stopped in front of a young captive. All the captives' hearts stopped beating. All eyes focussed on him. The eyes from the sack stared at the young man. The French officials waited for this moment; they watched the movement of the *bao bo*'s head. He nodded! Immediately the young captive was dragged away by the armed guards. My father heard an electric cry from the young man. He was not seen again.

The following morning, while being pushed out by two Vietnamese guards to the courtyard in front of a French official, my father decided he would say some words about himself to the French, no matter how hard the situation was.

'Je ne sais que servir l'église évangélique en remontant la vie spirituelle des fidèles,' my father quickly said as he passed the official. 'Je compte sur votre esprit de compréhension. . .' (literally, 'I only serve the Evangelical church and look after the spiritual life of the people. I plead for your understanding and. . .')

There was no response from the official. Instead, my father received some hard kicks from behind from the guards. The armed guards continued to push him further and further towards a small road running to an empty field behind several mounds of earth. He saw several captives with hands tied behind their backs and their eyes blindfolded. My father knew instantly what it was going to be. 'Father! Please take care of my wife and my children,' my father prayed.

One of the guards was about to put a bandage over my father's eyes. A French official was suddenly sighted running towards him waving a piece of paper.

'Etes-vous le pasteur, monsieur?' the frenchman breathlessly asked as he seized the guard's hands.

'Oui, monsieur. Je suis. . .'

The words stuck in my father's throat when the official showed him a piece of paper, the release order. Life had been exchanged for death at the last moment. My father saw it as a vindication of faith.

*　　　*　　　*

One evening, while the whole village was asleep, sounds of gunshots were heard, piercing the silence and breaking people's sleep. In the darkness of the house I heard my parents whisper something, then everything quickly returned to quietness. Early next morning, the sun rose up to reveal the body of a peasant woman with gunshot wounds. She lay exposed on the damp rice field, half her body sunk in the water and next to her a large bamboo basket full of buffalo meat. The woman had been shot dead by the soldier on guard from the night watchtower. News of the dead woman was whispered around the local market. She was from a nearby hamlet.

A group of French soldiers had surrounded her area the previous night to search for Viet minh, in order to take revenge for an attack on a French military post a few days before. No men were found because they had all run away hours before. Angrily, the French shot everything in sight, even a buffalo tied to the corner of a thatched hut. Unfortunately, the buffalo was the only means the dead woman and her family had to work in the fields.

The only thing this woman could do now was to sell its meat, new and fresh, to get the last benefit from the buffalo. She had hurriedly run across the rice fields before dawn to catch the early market. In the murky light of that morning, the tiny frame of the woman stooped under a heavy basket moving along the damp path became a target to be shot at by the soldier in the high watchtower.

From that day there was nothing beautiful left in the golden paddy fields I had treasured. The picture of the dead woman and the damp earth soaked with her blood haunted me day and night. The gold had been splashed forever with the red of suffering and horror.

3

Heads in the marketplace: 1946 – 1948

ON A DAY IN MID 1946, as usual, a group of peasant women left their remote village for the central market with their load of fresh countryside vegetables to sell. They were walking along the path amidst abundant paddy fields, chatting warmly to lighten their heavy burdens.

The fresh gentle breeze of the early morning fondled their faces, giving them new energy for the beginning of the day. The sweet scent of the ripening rice from the fields was everywhere. The women inhaled the scent through their lungs; it was like a kind of natural tonic, rich and healthy.

The newly-picked vegetables, green and crisp and piled in the large bamboo baskets, hung heavily on the carrying sticks suspended on their shoulders. Crunchy cucumbers, firm heavy pumpkins, green okra, shiny red tomatoes, crisp fresh spring onions, red hot chillies and countless other items all looked tempting, inviting people to enjoy the simplicity yet abundance of a country life.

It was not quite light yet. The women were still about twenty metres from the market. It seemed nobody was there yet. They thought they must be the first traders to arrive at the market that morning.

The woman walking in front suddenly stopped talking. Her eyes caught sight of something unusual in the middle of the marketplace. All of a sudden, she drew herself back as if hit by an electric shock. Her heavily-laden baskets swung back, smashing against her legs. 'What's that over there?' she screamed, burying her face in her hands. The others looked in the same direction.

'Oh my God! Oh my Buddha! Is it what we see?' they cried out, almost collapsing. In the morning gloom they saw the head of a person stuck on top of a bamboo stake set in the middle of the empty market! But not just one head — four — each on its stake! The bloody heads with dust-caked hair seemed like demons from hell, threatening.

'Who are they? What has happened to them? When did this occur?' The scene horrified the women. They stumbled over each other, turning in confusion and shock. Their vegetables scattered all over the place as they ran back, terrified, to their village.

The four men, it later became apparent, were suspected Viet minh and had been beheaded by the French at the village market. The news shocked the whole region and rapidly spread to other areas. The identity of these four men was never revealed to the villagers. Nobody knew who they were and what they had actually done to lead to such a savage execution. Nobody dared to come to the market. People were even afraid to openly discuss what had happened for fear of being mistakenly involved in these men's subversive actions.

For four days the market was empty and stark, like an open grave. There was not a living soul seen in the market. Only the four heads without bodies.

One night at midnight, through small gaps in the walls of their houses, the people living close to the market watched the French soldiers come in a military truck and take the stinking heads away. Some said they saw the heads put in a large bamboo basket full of sawdust. The next morning a notice board was set up in the market, calling for the market to return to normal. At the same time a reward was set for anyone who would tell the French the identity of the executed men.

The village market had always been a friendly place where the villagers happily met each other and made their living. It now became a place of stealth and suspicion. An eerie silence hovered over the whole area. Some women set in front of their goods a hand of fresh bananas and a burning incense stick as soon as they arrived at the market each morning. This small sign of worship was believed to ease the pain of the souls of those who had been beheaded.

My parents tried to keep knowledge of this terrible incident from us; yet somehow my eldest sister and I picked up everything from the whispered conversation of my parents' friends and neighbours. An old man sighed, 'God or Buddha must save us from the French!' He seemed sorry for his homeland being tortured by the invaders.

Another time a young man with his eyes sparkling with anger, said, 'The French or the *bao bo*?' He grimaced. 'Either must pay for their crimes one day! Especially the *bao bo*; I'm sure this is one of the results of their "loyalty" to the French.'

But outside, all remained silent! From that time, the front and backyard of our home became a ghostly area for me and my sisters every night. We dared not go outside in the evenings, even for a walk in the beautiful moonlight with my father.

This shocking event led my parents to make a very difficult decision — to move away from this place for their peace of mind, especially for their young children's well-being.

We had been living in a village about a two-hour bicycle ride from the centre of Saigon. Though this area was on the edge of the city, its lifestyle had been that of the countryside, possessing its own rural character. This was neither my father's native village nor my mother's; but my father had been working with the church in this area for many years.

Life had become more difficult every day. My father struggled to keep the church's people together; but they kept leaving for more remote areas, isolated hamlets where they considered it safer. Some had moved even to far provinces.

One day my father told us that he had discussed with my uncles, Dan and Son, about our family joining their families in Cambodia for a more secure life. Dan is my mother's eldest brother and Son the husband of my mother's twin sister. Everything seemed to be worked out well between my father and uncles.

My father decided that he would send my mother and us children to stay in Phnom Penh for a period of time. He believed it would be safer for us there. The plan also included my aunt Sa and her family, my grandmother, and some other family members. Sa is my mother's twin sister. Some close friends of my uncle also took a similar decision for their families.

My father decided to stay with the church, no matter how few people remained. My parents were sad at having to make this heart-breaking decision. For the first time they were going to live apart. The move would mean many other serious changes, especially for my mother, a young woman with four little children. Leaving my father alone was another matter of concern.

'Are there Viet minh in Phnom Penh, Papa?' my eldest sister asked when we were having tea at the table one evening. It shocked my mother to hear the word 'Vietminh' come from the mouth of her nine-year-old daughter.

Frightened, my mother put her hand over my sister's mouth. 'Oh my little darling, don't you dare say that word again, especially outside in the street. Try hard to remember this, dear — or your papa could be in trouble.' She gave my father a concerned look — she could not believe how little children could pick up these secret things!

But my father seemed very calm. He said, 'Of course not, my dear. Viet minh are Vietnamese. They are not in Cambodia.'

I was always the shy girl in the family, though I wanted to ask, 'Why do we have to go to Phnom Penh? We are also Vietnamese!'

The breeze lingered in the golden blossom trees blooming that January. At last my mother began to pack things for the journey. It was early spring, 1948. The signs of the Lunar New Year — 'Tet' — were felt and seen everywhere — the coolness in the air, the flocks of swallows chirping under the clear blue sky, some early blooms of 'Mai' (golden in the south and pink in the north), the traditional Tet flower which people believed would bring good luck and fortune to the family.

In the Vietnamese tradition, Tet is the most inspiring time of the year for individuals and families. It is the opportunity for a new beginning and new hope for life, for sharing and for happiness. The moment of time between the old and new year is the time for the burning of sweet incense to those who have passed away and for picking the very first Mai blossoms in the hope that the best dreams would come true, traditions that have kept family bonds strong. Carrying out these customs is flesh and blood; without them life is empty and dead.

But we did not bother to think of such loving traditions of Tet. Now life was forcing many people to separate from their loved ones, breaking the spirit of union and love which always drew families together at new year. This sense of separation was as true for my family as for others. It was made more poignant when, a few months later, I found out that my mother was expecting another baby.

*   *   *

It was still early, but I was already awake. On the deck of the boat I saw almost everybody from our extended family. I re-called how busy the previous night was at the wharf, and the anxious call from my grandmother to my uncle Son, aunt Sa's husband, to check on the children, to make sure they all were on board. It took an hour for our family finally to settle down on deck with all our luggage. Now all were soundly asleep, except uncle Son. He was sitting quietly, facing the deck rail with his legs hanging over the side. I guessed he was resting, enjoying the freshness and quietness of an early morning on the river.

The ship was moving slowly. I crawled a little towards the edge of the deck and looked into the water. Little waves were constantly lapping against the side of the boat, stirring the water and making beautiful white foam. I laughed softly to myself, because I thought perhaps the ship was having a morning shave, with real foam washed off by the river. I looked a little further out through the deck rail to a large fishing boat where a woman stood cleaning her teeth. She turned her face upwards with the toothbrush running rapidly along her teeth; then she swirled the bubbles noisily in her mouth and spat into the water.

For the first time I was on a boat leaving Vietnam. As a little girl I thought it would be an endless journey. A few days earlier I had seen my grandmother busily preparing a lot of dried food for this trip: rice rolls, meat and fish flake, boiled salted duck eggs, dried bananas, home-made ginger marmalade, and drinking water.

I did not realise until later that the food was prepared for only two days, the time for the boat to reach its destination. But we were nine children and seven adults in all, a large group of people, and we would consume a lot. We were on the open deck — the cheapest priced area, my uncle explained to me. I liked this place because the fresh air came across the open deck most of the day. I did not feel seasick as I would have had I been sitting in a cabin.

The ship carried about 100 passengers including children. All were sleeping. Their heads moved slightly from side to side with the vibration of the ship's engine. On both sides of the ship's bow I saw two huge eyes painted in red and black. The ship's eyes really looked as if they were real. I did not know whether these eyes were painted on most vessels as a decoration, or to threaten the sea-devils in a superstitious way.

Everything suddenly had gone into the past. There was the picture of my father standing at the station in Saigon waving the last goodbye to us as the bus was disappearing. I remember when the driver's assistant suddenly urged all the passengers to get on the bus. My father quickly hopped on to find our seats for us. Then we were safe in there with all the hand luggage. The noisy sounds from the bus engine reminded people it was time to leave. Half the time I shed copious tears, hiding my face in my mother's dress, while for the other half I looked out the bus window to find my father in the crowd.

'Be good, my little girls! I'll see you and your mother soon in Phnom Penh!' my father shouted out from the crowd. He stretched his hand over other people to hold my mother's. Silence spoke more than a thousand words at that moment.

The bus driver anxiously finished off the last goodbyes from the passengers and their families as he shouted warmly, 'Pay me again and I'll bring these people back to you. Easy! Don't worry!'

I pictured our home village which had become a fearful memory where I knew my father had to live in an empty house alone.

I could also picture my aunt's house in Tan Chau in which we stayed for one month before we all left for Phnom Penh. It was in the district of Chau Doc, a small province about 250 kilometres west of Saigon, near Cambodia. In those days, the local people specialised in raising silkworms to produce silk and, after using them for their best silk, the silkworms became a 'yummy' snack for children when boiled with a little salt. When the seller opened her deep bamboo basket covered with a thick layer of banana leaves, I remember how the steam of newly boiled silkworms and their natural brilliant yellow colour really tempted the other children and me.

And now we were travelling up the Mekong River, the way into Cambodia. I was obsessed with the pain of being too far away from my father. When would I see him again?

Cambodia in 1945 had fallen under French colonial rule along with Vietnam and Laos; whereas Burma and Malaya had been occupied by the British. Many people from Vietnam had fled to Cambodia or Laos to find security because of the fear of savage terrorism between the French and the anti-French Viet minh movement.

The city of Phnom Penh lies along the west side of the Bassac River where it joins the Mekong River. The Bassac has the unusual feature that for half of the year it flows towards the sea, while for the other half of the year it reverses the flow and goes to the large inland sea of Tonle Sap.

There did not seem to be many middle-class Cambodians around Phnom Penh — they were mostly labourers, peddlers and beggars. There is a saying that 'Anywhere that has smoke has Chinese', and I remember seeing Chinese everywhere I went in town. Many shops in the heart of Phnom Penh were run by them. As we lived in a city that was full of French, Chinese and Vietnamese, we did not have much chance to make friends with the Cambodian people, except for our maid. She was a pleasant teenage girl. I remember after the short sleep following lunch, the maid used to buy lotus buds for us from the Cambodian peddler as an afternoon refreshment.

There were quite a few Vietnamese families living around town. Even the Cambodian peddlers knew how to call out 'lotus buds' in Vietnamese — *Bup sen day*! 'Bup' actually has a high tone, but they tended to make it a low tone. Eventually it became a beguiling signal of wake-up time for us each afternoon when they passed our area. The lotus was very common in this land.

I learnt how to eat lotus seeds from the buds. They are white, brittle seeds, the size of one's finger joint. Each white seed is covered by a light green, thick, soft skin. These seeds are hidden inside the bud, a funnel-like soft husk with a long strong stalk. The seeds can be seen as little dark dots scattered on the surface of the green bud. No great effort is needed to get to the seeds. It only takes a second; but it is fun and they are good to eat. The stamen is the bitter part that needs to be taken out before eating.

The significance of the lotus is not only in its beauty, but also in its contributing its all to our everyday use — the flowers, seeds, stalks, leaves and roots. One 'magic' characteristic of the lotus leaf is that if a live eel is wrapped in a leaf, the eel becomes absolutely immobile until you take it home from the market and unwrap it. The countryside people can never explain why, but it works wonders.

In Asian culture, the lotus flower is the symbol of goodness, purity and modesty. It is the symbol of *quan tu* — a good man. Though from the bottom of the mud, it becomes beautiful and benefits people.

Soon all the children became attached to the maid. We called her 'Xiem' (pronounced 'seem'), imitating the sound of her Cambodian name which we never knew exactly. The maid was not a luxury. We were a large family with many children, and the adults needed a hand with the housework so that they could help run our medicine shop more effectively.

After dinner, Xiem used to take us across our street to a public park for a walk or to play games. Our different languages and skin colour did not trouble us. We talked, laughed and teased each other. I found it the most pleasant time of the day. The only thing we did not like was that she liked to flavour our soups with a little *mam bo hoc*, a traditional Cambodian preserved food made with fish. My grandmother was really annoyed about it. It is made in a similar way to traditional Vietnamese *nuoc mam*, fish sauce, but *mam bo hoc* is much stronger.

The two-storey house we shared in Phnom Penh during this time was one of the French-styled brick terrace houses in Odier Street, one of the busiest streets of the city. Early in the morning, I usually saw huge fresh sea fish brought from the river being carried across the street in front of our house to the central food market. From our place, we could easily walk to the city shopping area where my uncle used to take all the children to a movie at the Eden cinema.

Tarzan was the very first movie I saw in my life. I remember the scene of Tarzan's beautiful wife wearing a green unsewn dress, sitting by a stream full of white water lilies. Though I was only a little girl, I was enraptured by such a peaceful life that could only be a dream.

The Chinese medicine shop run by my two uncles occupied almost the entire ground floor of the house. A wall and a side door divided the kitchen and other family facilities. A stair from the kitchen led to the second floor which was used as the sleeping place for the whole family.

The shop had quite a large range of traditional remedies made into powder, tablets, pills, ointments and plasters for all common sicknesses, including pregnancy. These were delivered to the shop from a Chinese wholesale dealer. Most of our medicines were the products of Vo Dinh Dan, a very popular trusted name in Chinese medicines. A Chinese medicine doctor — he was actually a Vietnamese, a friend of our family — was also invited to work at the shop once a week to see patients.

The Oriental medicine doctors are men of wisdom. Their knowledge of feeling the pulse and listening to the harmony of the human body to distinguish the different sicknesses that occur fascinated me. A quiet place, a few minutes uninterrupted, and a soft small cushion for the patient's hand to lean on: these are all he needs to examine a patient.

Generally the right hand pulse is the main spot to be examined. The patient puts the hand with the palm up on the cushion; then the doctor gently puts the three middle fingers of his right hand on the patient's wrist towards the right edge and presses. The pulse gently pumps up and down under his fingers. There he feels and reads everything inside the body — sick or healthy, wrong or right, common or serious; the pulse indicates it very clearly by the rhythm.

His mastery of the use of Oriental medicinal herbs also fascinated me. There are not five or ten, but thousands of them. But he knows the significant character of each and the effective combination between them, in order to make wonder-ful remedies to heal people. It could cause instant death if the herbs are mixed wrongly. But I have not heard of any death caused by taking herbs mixed incorrectly.

I remember how I felt when I looked into a bowl of *thuoc bac* or 'northern medicine' — it originally came south from northern Vietnam — and drank it: the dark liquid extract of mixed herbs looked like hell and taking it was certainly like falling into hell when its bitter taste touched my tongue and my throat. But afterwards I felt the precious goodness of nature running through my body as an assurance of good health again.

My two uncles managed the shop and the women of the family took turns to serve the shop's customers every day as well as look after the housework. This business was the joint effort of three families, so in thirds everything was shared between them. However, my grandmother seemed like the soul of all three families. She strongly involved herself in everything from the shop to the kitchen, from the customers to each family member, from our business to the family's personal affairs.

In front of our medicine shop, a young northern Vietnamese man hired the corner of the right side to use as his work station. He made his living by doing embroidery. Every day, from the minute he came, he simply sat on a high stool, placed his standing embroidering frame close in front of him, then constantly needled over a complicated pattern with colourful threads. Next to him was a large canvas handbag full of threads and patterns. Some patterns were nearly torn apart along the pencil lines by being used many times.

His delicate skill soon became well-known. It specially attracted the wives of many French officials living and working in town. Many people ordered embroidery on dresses, blouses, tablecloths and napkins. This made him extremely busy from morning to evening.

It was fascinating to watch him work. He had a big ball of used candle wax; sometimes he ran a thread over the wax to avoid it being entangled. A pair of scissors was there, but he always used his teeth to bite the unwanted knots on the threads. He worked so hard that it seemed he was not aware of my presence next to him. Suddenly he would stop and smile at me. 'Would you mind if I ask for a little fresh water to drink?' he paused for one second, looked into our house and then whispered to me, 'Only if your granny is not there, dear!' And I ran and got him a little fresh water which I thought he really appreciated.

Soon afterwards, my Aunt Sa opened a fresh flower stand at the left corner alongside this man's stall, mainly to attract the French living locally and others whose social lives were associated with them.

Later, when I looked back on this time, I thought it could have been a good opportunity for my relatives to become well-off, as there were many trading possibilities around the front of the medicine shop. Somehow it did not work out well for my relatives' families.

My eldest sister and I were sent to a Vietnamese primary school together with my two cousins. The Mekong Primary School was four small rooms of bamboo-thatched roof and wall, and dirt floor; three were used as classrooms and one as a school office. There were about fifty children aged from seven to ten and three Vietnamese teachers. One was a middle-aged man with glasses; he was also the school principal.

I have never forgotten the dry dusty surrounds of the school. No grass, no trees, no flower bushes, not even a fence line. All was a large dirt yard. When the children played rope-jumping it was a real disaster!

At school break-time, a Chinese man came regularly to sell home-made ice-cream to the children. He had two big wooden buckets. I did not know how he managed to bring them from his home to our school each day. He also had about four or five glass bottles which contained different mixed liquids such as orange syrup, lemon juice and coconut milk with sugar.

In one bucket coated with a thick rug and rice husks at the bottom, he put a lot of broken ice mixed with rock salt; then he poured the liquid into many round tinned tubes, and dropped in each a split bamboo stick as an ice-cream handle. Finally he carefully placed all the tubes in the bucket among the ice and salt, covered them with a thick piece of canvas, and waited until the liquids froze. He must have made them about two hours beforehand.

To sell them, he collected the children's money; then he took several tubes by holding the end of the bamboo sticks, shook the ice off the tubes by partly soaking them in the other bucket containing fresh water, and gave them to the children. In fact it was only ice made just above zero so that it would not be as hard as ice. But I remember that in the hot sun all the children were dying for this ice-cream from the dear old Chinese. He was so friendly and sometimes did not even bother to collect the money from the children if there was only a little left in the bucket. I loved sucking the juicy coconut milk coming out of the soft ice. He certainly made a small world happy.

It was a Vietnamese school with Vietnamese teachers and pupils, but each day we began our study by standing up to greet the teacher when he or she first came into the class. '*Asseyez-vous!*,' 'Sit down,' the teacher said. Then all the class would say together with a rhythm, '*Nous nous asseyons à la classe*,' 'We all sit down in the classroom.'

Every subject used French, though the lessons were written in Vietnamese. Even things to use in class were also said in French. In the higher classes, French lessons took four to five hours per week.

The pupils were not allowed to speak Vietnamese in these lessons. At the beginning of class, the teacher would open the roll and call, for example, Nguyen Van Anh. He would answer in French, 'Present'. We all gradually learnt some French and automatically mixed it with our Vietnamese.

This obligatory but lax system meant many could only speak broken French. They were cheated of being 'sophisticated', which created pressures amongst the less and more sophisticated French speakers.

There was a larger primary school close to the Mekong school. It provided a 'pure' French educational system. It was for children from rich families and was strongly influenced by the French. I remember seeing the children, whose faces were Asian — they could be Cambodian, Chinese or Vietnamese. They were always well dressed and spoke French everywhere, and seemed very proud of being pupils of the French school, of being able to speak the most prestigious language. Constant fights and arguments erupted among the children of the two schools along the way home after school because of what appeared to be pride on one side and resentment on the other.

I had conflicting feelings of being a slave under the French, yet of having the desire to learn to speak their 'most civilised' language. This confused me for much of my teen-age years. I thought if I tried to master the French language and use it to earn my living, would I still be considered a patriot? Or would people think of me as a kind of traitor?

Our school was far from our home. It took us about an

hour to walk to school and back home every day. All the children had to attend both morning and afternoon study sessions. It was very hard for children, but that was the educational system applied in schools in those days.

My mother told my eldest sister that the family joint budget could not extend to us going to school by 'cyclo' — trishaw — every day, though they knew the school was not close to our home. But if it was raining or we were not feeling well, we could take a cyclo home and they would pay for us.

One day we were tired and bored as we went home. I insisted that we take a cyclo for a change. Several of them always parked in the street waiting for passengers. Immediately we hopped on one, two sitting on the laps of the other two. The driver was an old Cambodian man. He was thin and weak. He tried to hold down the vehicle while we struggled to squeeze ourselves in a narrow seat which was only used for one person. We did not speak a word of Cambodian to explain that we could not afford to go in two cyclos.

The poor old man struggled for a while to get the vehicle balanced then off he went. I guessed he was also in need of money. All our pointing was something like tangled wool; but we reached home eventually.

'Who allowed you to take a cyclo home?' our grandma asked, angrily twisting my sister's blouse. My sister looked upon me as her rescuer for a proper answer. We did not want to say it was our mother. 'It was me, grandma!' I said. 'My tummy was upset!' I lied to my grandmother to rescue my sister.

'Then only rice soup tonight and a tablet as well.' I was hungry and longed for a good meal as usual; but I held my tears back as I determined to save my sister from my grandmother's anger. My mother did not know what was happening to us as she was so busy with the evening customers in the shop.

That night, my sister took me to the bathroom. She gave me a lolly and flushed the diarrhea tablet she had got from my grandma for me into the toilet. When my sister kissed me, I felt the wetness of her cheeks. We both felt like we were orphans, lonely and hungry.

When I grew up a little, I realised that my grandmother's overbearing nature had caused severe distress in our family. Her aggressive manner caused the marriage break-up of her eldest son, Dan. In an Asian family, the eldest son assumes the responsibility for the parents, whether they are still alive or even after death. Dan took up this responsibility not only as his duty, but also with loving care. But he also cared for his wife in a special way.

The two women became jealous of each other. Both demanded a unique place in his life. But a common saying explained what was in the minds of most old people: 'One can find another wife easily, but not other parents.' After his wife left him with some of their children, Dan never found the same happiness again. My grandmother refused the help of our family's close friends for a reconciliation. She honestly believed, I am sure, that she was the most caring person in the family.

I remember one day the Chinese medicine doctor was about half-an-hour late because his bicycle had a flat tyre on the way to our shop. There were several patients with common complaints waiting for him inside our shop. My grandmother became restless. She walked up and down in the tiny area which was used as the doctor's office. She was constantly fanning herself with a paper fan. Suddenly the doctor walked in, carrying with him a box of Chinese tea. He handed over the tea he had bought for my grandmother as a gift and, with a caring friendly smile he said, 'Here Mama, it's for you!'

'It's not mama or papa at the moment,' she shouted to the doctor. 'It's the patients. Don't you care?' She hit the doctor's hand and the box dropped on the floor.

The doctor, a loyal friend of Dan's, felt like he had fallen from heaven to hell. Later he decided to stay full-time at his own shop. After that, our shop lost a lot of customers.

Soon after that, the new baby arrived to join us. The joy of having the first boy in the family brought my father to visit Phnom Penh. He even bought a birth gift for my baby brother, a gold bracelet with his name engraved on it.

I remember several comments from my parents' friends up to this time when my parents were asked how many children of each sex they had. All girls! The attitude of my parents' friends seemed very negative. 'Then who cares for both of you in your old age? All the girls will belong to the others. Try again!' In the carefree atmosphere of our own family, my parents enjoyed their girls and had never complained of having no boys. However, the new baby boy had brought a new joy and great excitement for them. After that, another girl and three boys were added to make nine in our family.

Though the baby was only one month old, my parents took him with us and, together with our relatives, we visited many places in Cambodia, such as Angkor Wat and Angkor Thom. Later we also had a chance to visit Kampot where we stayed with the family of a Vietnamese missionary to the Cambodians.

Though in a happy frame of mind, my eldest sister did not forget to tell my father how miserable we felt when we lived apart from him. 'If you could find a different house in Saigon we would not feel scared to live there, Papa!'

'You're right, my dear! I will soon!' He embraced all

of us and said, 'You know how much I miss all of you!'

'Do you miss Mama also, Papa?' my younger sister suddenly asked.

'Yes, dear! Very much!' My parents gazed at each other and smiled. A tenderness sparkled in their eyes; but I knew they would never express their affection to each other publicly.

*　　　*　　　*

One of the letters, which my father wrote to my mother after he returned to Vietnam, said: '. . .There are not many church activities these days; instead, together with our friends and neighbours, I often have to flee from home to a remote bush village to hide from random security checks for a few days or a week. When news comes that it is safe to come back to the village, then I come back home. I often have Canh as my "running" companion to hide in the bush. He always carries with him a bag containing a box of green tea, a kettle and some tea cups, some rice and dried fish. When we settle in a place, he collects some wood, makes a stove by digging a small hole in the dirt, then boils water to make tea.

'On one occasion, he sat down on a cluster of broken cement graves, invited me for a cup of hot tea while anxiously sipping his and said, "I don't think of this as miserable at all. In fact, I'm glad the French dare not to come to this area."' And my father concluded his letter by saying, 'I'm afraid I won't be able to arrange a new place for you before next Christmas.'

This thought fascinated me so much — it must have been so exciting there!

*　　　*　　　*

My sister took me along with her to a French bakery around the corner to buy bread for our family Christmas Eve celebration. My mother and my aunt had been busy preparing food for that night. The evening of December 24 is important — the main Christmas celebration takes place in most churches and in homes afterwards. December 25 is a rest day.

Along Odier Street I counted that eight out of ten houses had a Christmas tree with beautiful decorations on it. The only fine bakery in town was packed with people rushing about the last few hours before it was closed. Golden roasted turkeys on trays, cold meat and gelatins of all kinds, large and small *Bûche de Noël* and home-made cookies were available. Most of the shop's customers were French women, there were some Vietnamese and a few Cambodians. The Chinese seemed to stick to their tradition of Lunar Calendar New Year more than Christmas. People had more or less adapted to the French lifestyle, though not all of them were Christians.

The hot stuffy atmosphere in our house caused by too much cooking, too much talking and laughing and too many people gathering in such a limited area made me feel sick all evening after we came back from church. We all sat down at the table for the Christmas evening meal.

My mind went back to the rural village where I imagined that my father was hiding from the French, sitting on the broken cement grave sipping his green tea, celebrating a Christmas without a family, or a church. A lonely shepherd in the desert. I whispered to myself, 'I miss you, Papa!'

*　　　*　　　*

'I'm going back home! I'm going back home! Saigon! Saigon!'

The joy of returning home seemed to stretch its wings in me to carry all the love and affection from a little girl back to her home before she was able to reach there herself. It sounded strange to me when I repeated the idea in my mind, but it was really true!

I was about to get on the bus. All the different sounds

and noises at the station did not bother me. My grandmother, my aunts, my cousins, goodbye! My school and my little friends, goodbye! The public park and the cement bench where my sister and I used to take a rest on the way home after school, goodbye! The maid, the lotus lady and the ice-cream man, goodbye! Goodbye to you all! Believe it or not, I'm going home! I felt as if I could take a giant step and cross the border and within a minute I would see my father in reality.

The bus was crowded with men, women and children. Everybody looked happy and friendly. 'They're going home with me also,' I thought. The roof was crammed with luggage, packs, sacks and bags. Lots of specialities from Phnom Penh would be nice gifts to families — sugar palm, dried lotus seeds, dried salted sea fish and shrimps which were very popular as traditional delicious food and cheap to buy because Phnom Penh has the benefit of being close to the inner sea Tonle Sap.

My uncle Son beamed at me when he carried me over the steps to get on the bus. 'See, my dear! I have chosen the best bus for you!' It was really a brand new bus painted in bright red. The seats inside were clean and shining. My mother looked happy. She would feel much better with her little boy in these spacious seats.

The trip by bus from Phnom Penh to Saigon takes about seven hours. My uncle Son was to help to escort us from Phnom Penh to Svay Rieng on the border. This meant that we would have already gone two-thirds of the journey, and from there my uncle would leave us and return to Phnom Penh.

The strong wind that blew back from both sides of the bus almost choked me, twirling my sister's long hair. Going, going. . . all the trees and the electricity poles along the road quickly disappeared behind me. One, two, three, four. . . I tried to count them one by one until I felt breathless and they became something very vague like a wall of dust.

Soon we reached Neak Luong. The sun was high in the sky, the hottest time of the day. The bus stopped. Our bus emptied quickly, except for some women and children, including my mother and us. 'Mia, mia day! Khom ngot day! Chuoi kho day! Ca phe da day!' The noisy excited invitations were competing with each other from the street vendors, women and children, for us to buy little snacks and refreshments such as sugarcane cut in stems, pineapples eyed and cut into pieces, dried bananas, even ready-made coffee with ice — all the sounds assaulted my ears. A little boy with a large bamboo tray of sugarcane stems planted firmly on top of his head hopped on the bus steps. 'Mia ngot, mia ngot day!', 'Sweet sugarcane here'. He then hopped out.

It was then I noticed Uncle Son was missing. 'What's wrong, Mama?'

'Can you see the big river over there?' My mother pointed towards a large expanse of water. 'We have to cross the river by ferry. The passengers are not allowed to sit on the bus when crossing the river on a ferry; only women with young children.'

'Has uncle left us?' I asked, worried.

'No, we'll meet him at the other side of the river.' It seemed a good time for everybody to stretch their legs and do a little exercise after sitting still for hours in the bus.

My mother took from a canvas bag a baby milk bottle which had some mixed condensed milk and boiled water in it. It was time to feed the baby. My mother suddenly said to my eldest sister, 'Poor grandma! She'll miss us!'

She looked into the bag. There were some sticky rice rolls and meat flake. There was a tin of Tiger Balm heat cream named Masphsu, originally from Burma with the registered logo, the picture of a Burmese lady. There was also the Two Heaven Ointment, a product of China. These are among the traditional 'pocket remedies' which help to relieve such common symptoms as headache, dizziness, vomiting or even a minor cut or a bite from insects. All that is needed is to apply it around the nose, temples, chest or on the trouble spot. It is also used as an inhalant. I find it works wonderfully. But I do not know whether people really feel an effective result in using it or is it a mother's love that does it all?

'These ointments are really needed when you're going on a long journey. Especially with small children.' My mother recalled these words from my grandmother when she had prepared for her trip the previous day.

Our bus finally drove onto the ferry, along with some cars. The passengers clustered around their vehicles on board. The ferry, heavily laden with passengers and vehicles full of luggage, left the wharf and headed towards the other side of the river. The picture of all the peddlers standing along the riverbank became smaller and smaller and finally disappeared from my sight. Not a breath of wind stirred the river.

'Here's uncle again!' My mother cheered up the baby by holding him high through the bus window. It took about three-quarters-of-an-hour to cross the river. Everybody got back on the bus and the journey continued to Svay Rieng. I remember the bus left the Phnom Penh station at half past nine that morning, though we had to get up at six o'clock to get everything ready. It was now about half past twelve. Both driver and passengers needed a lunch break; it would last about half-an-hour. Then there was only around another three hours and we would arrive in Saigon.

'Well, sister!' My uncle Son called to my mother after we came back from the shop where we had been eating. 'Sorry I'm not able to go all the way with you and the children. But I'm sure you're safe from here.' He kissed my sisters and me. 'You'll see Papa soon. Send my regards to Papa, will you?' Then he said goodbye to my mother and hurried to cross the road to catch a return bus to go back to Phnom Penh.

Our bus travelled fast and soon Cu Chi came into view. We were now within Vietnam, about 130 kilometres north-west of Saigon. The bus suddenly slowed down as if it were going to stop. The engine sounded normal. It was not a flat tyre because that would shake the bus. 'What's going on, driver?' a man's voice shouted anxiously from the back of the bus. The driver did not answer. 'Is the stupid bus not going, man? Do you know what is happening?' an old man called gruffly.

Silence! The driver looked frightened. His eyes stared at something in the distance, in the dry paddy fields off the road. Something was wrong. He had travelled on this road for a long time and he had enough experience to know that the figures on the roadside were not the types of passengers who were late and tried to catch the last bus. They looked unusual. Black peasant outfits, lantana leaf hats — and something else!

'Oh no! It's the Viet minh! It's them, for sure!' the driver cried out fearfully. He pressed his foot hard on the accelerator to make the bus jump up instantly to a hundred kilometres per hour.

'Stop the bus, driver! Stop! I said stop!' the big man from the back and his friend shouted to the driver. They had guns in their hands. Everybody was shocked.

Immediately my mother pushed us down under the seat. She stooped down to cover her little boy. My sisters and I were terrified. My eldest sister pushed me down harder and screamed, 'Will you be all right, Mama?' Our little brother started to cry out loudly. He had been pressed too hard to my mother's chest.

'Heads down, everybody! Shut your baby up, will you?' they yelled out to the passengers and to my mother.

The bus stopped as ordered. From the open windows of the bus the two men fired clusters of gunshots into the fields. The Viet minh fired back. Their bullets hit the left side of the bus like a rain of hailstones. The fight between the two Vietnamese French security police who happened to be passengers of this bus and the Viet minh guerrilla group continued fiercely for five or six minutes.

All of a sudden, one of the security police dropped his gun; a bullet coming through the window hit his right arm and went through the other side. 'Move on, driver! Quick! Move on!' the other man ordered. The Viet minh guerrillas probably did not realise how small the fighting force was on the bus, whereas they were a group of five or six. The bus started moving. No more gunshots came from the fields. The guerillas quietly ran away alongside the fields and disappeared.

Fortunately, the security policeman had only a minor wound to his arm. He used his handkerchief as a bandage to tie around it. Although a little pale, he looked proud of what he had done. The two of them considered themselves the victors.

Nobody else on the bus was hurt or wounded. A night-mare was just over. We all got back on the seats extremely bewildered. My mother's hand was still shaking when she touched each of us on the face. She said, 'Thank God you're still all right!' A Catholic woman next to my mother made the sign of the cross, her closed eyes blinking rapidly.

The bus was now like a wounded animal with all the bullet marks deep and shallow in its side. The bus angrily jumped up and down on the rugged road until signs of Saigon city appeared.

Some passengers blamed the security police for their extreme action, and that they did not worry about the lives of the passengers. 'What did the police mean by doing that?' a man said. 'Was it just to show off their power? There were only two of them.' They mocked, 'That's how he's been wounded!'

Others seemed negative. 'The Viet minh probably planned a quiet attack to take our possessions for their needs, that's all.' And they concluded, 'It's certainly like taking a poisonous serpent home to kill their own chicken!', a Vietnamese saying.

All the women were thankful that the brand new bus had a strong body so that the bullets could not break through.

*   *   *

'Here's your ice-cream, darlings!' my father called to us from the crowd at the Saigon bus station. I burst into tears and the ice-cream dropped when my father held us all in his arms.

4

Viet minh terrorist on the run: 1948

'Merci bien pour votre franchise. Mais je suis sûr que monsieur Hoa n'est pas là!', 'I appreciate your honesty. But I know very well Mr Hoa is not there!'

The French sûreté stressed the words 'merci bien' with disappointment, as if he hoped my father had not been so innocent in this matter.

My father slowly got out of the truck and stepped into his house, dazed and very confused. It was only 2.30 a.m. Most Saigon people were sound asleep. In the quietness of the night, my father could still hear the groan of the French security officer's truck as it angrily turned the corner down the road as my father shut the front door behind him.

'You're back? Oh, thank God!' It was a surprise to see my father back so soon. My mother stared at him. 'Thank God! I sat here and prayed for you from the moment you left with them. You look exhausted!' My mother went to the kitchen and brought my father a cool drink. Her happy attitude suddenly evaporated.

'Darling, was Hoa there at his home? Is he. . .?' Her eyes in the flicker of the night candle glistened as if they were set in pools of tears. My mother believed that Hoa had been arrested; otherwise the sûreté would not have let my father come back home.

'No, he was not there. I prayed hard on the way to his place that he would not be there!' The flame, twinkling again, lit up the confusion on my father's face. 'But it was hard to explain to Hoa's wife why I took the French to their home. Of course I didn't want Hoa to be in trouble. But what would they think if I had said I don't know where he lives? He's my brother.'

For hours my parents sat in silence turning over in their minds the unbelievable news about my uncle Hoa. . .

A few days before, my uncle had had an upsetting argument with my mother. Hoa had rushed home one morning while my mother was busy with her housework. My father was out.

'Sister!' Hoa called my mother from his bedroom. 'Can you lend me some money right away? I definitely need it.'

'What's it for?' my mother shouted from the kitchen, surprised.

'I'll explain later. I'll pay you back later, sister.'

'But you know very well I don't have any money. Can you wait for your brother?'

Hoa came out of his room holding his packed briefcase. He sat down on a stool to put his shoes on. He looked tired and shabby. 'Sister, can you lend me your gold wedding ring? I'll sell it. I'll return a new one to you soon. I promise!'

My mother stared at him. Never before had he been like this. 'What's wrong with you, Hoa? Can you tell me?' He stood up. He looked out the front door. 'Don't you want to help? Tell me, are you going to lend me your ring or will I go right now?'

My mother's face blanched and her lips quivered. Hoa did not wait for her answer. He ran to the door and stood there angrily, shouting back into the house to my mother and swearing loudly to the great surprise of our neighbours. Then he disappeared.

It was shortly after this that the French security officer came to see Papa. 'Your brother is suspected of being a Viet minh. Are you aware of this?' The officer swept the torch over the arrest order which he was showing my father, and said he was told that Hoa had been staying with him.

Confused, my father answered, 'It's true that he was with us. But he just left us a few days ago!'

'Why did he leave you?' The French officer again waved the torch around the house suspiciously.

'That's also my concern, monsieur!' The upset caused by my uncle suddenly leaving our house was still fresh in our minds. My father paused for a moment then continued. 'He had a big argument with my wife over something small while I was not at home. He moved out straight after that.'

'Where is he now?'

'He said he would go back to his wife. That's all we know.'

The officer's response was immediate. He ordered my father to take him and his team to the place which was supposed to be his brother's home. It was a little after midnight. My father asked for one minute to get dressed.

'Will everything be all right?' my mother whispered to my father in the bedroom.

'Pray for me, darling!'

My father knew it was not wise to express any of his thoughts to my mother at that moment because the two Vietnamese police were in the front room. Quietly he slipped off his wedding ring, left it on the night table, together with his watch and his wallet. Then he hurried out and left with the French officer and his team.

After many years of living in unsettled situations, leaving those small personal possessions with my mother had become an indication of how serious he thought the crisis could be. 'It helps you, though only a little, in case I don't come back. I can't use them in prison anyway. In fact I may lose them,' he explained.

My father felt like a criminal! How many more times was this going to happen to him? It was a disgrace for the Vietnamese to be ruled brutally by foreigners within their homeland. The French had grown more and more concerned about the Viet minh — the anti-French national group — and this fear threatened the lives of innocent people.

His memories went back to the time when he missed the compulsory draw lots for Vietnamese men aged from twenty-one to twenty-five to join the army. Each year the French chose a number of young men by drawing their names by lots. They would be sent somewhere in France for short-term basic military training, then return to Vietnam to serve in the French army against their compatriots. What would have happened if his name had been drawn and he had become, like others, an enemy of his homeland? People had heard about the Viet minh and secretly admired them. But to my father it needed 'more birds in the sky before the weather would change to Spring'.

Many traumatic matters flooded my father's mind — conflicting feelings about a brother who had committed his life to love, honesty and justice. 'Is he really a Viet minh? It's hard to believe!' my father thought — and then: 'He's not all that bad. . . In fact, he's to be admired!'

For a while my father closed his eyes and let his mind picture what God might do to help.

'Which direction, monsieur?' one of the Vietnamese police shouted, thrusting the cold hard gun barrel against my father's shoulder.

'To Phu Nhuan,' came the automatic answer. Sweat ran down my father's forehead.

In fact Hoa did not have his own home. Since he had married Dao Buu Lan, an attractive girl from a Chinese-Vietnamese family who had been going to the same church as he did in the Saigon area, he had moved in and shared the house with her parents and brother. Everything went well at the beginning; but later Hoa's life became unsettled, leading him to make this request of my parents: 'If both you and brother are kind enough to let me stay here for a few months, I would appreciate it very much! I must try hard this time to find a place of my own for my wife and the two children. I find it so hard to face my mother-in-law at present, so I don't visit often, even though Lan and the children are still there.'

The sadness and disappointment expressed in the dark eyes of my young uncle, who as a child was an orphan cared for by my mother for several years, touched her heart. She was as concerned for him now as she had been in the days when he was still a small child in her family. And so my mother talked to my father about giving him temporary shelter in our home.

At that time our home was located on a large new residential development very close to Saigon. It had been known as Khu Vuon Chuoi, the banana orchard area. Up until the fall of Saigon it was one of the busiest inner town areas of Saigon with a large number of city dwellers, an abundant daily food market and plenty of trading shops and other businesses.

Our house was fifteen metres long and six metres wide with a dirt floor and a palm-leaf roof. The walls were made of clay mixed with straw and painted with white lime water. It was a simple design with a living and family room across the front of the house and three other small rooms on one side, leaving a narrow passage from front to back down the other side.

These rooms were used as bedrooms, as well as having other functions. The very small kitchen opened into the backyard where there was a small washing area. The toilet and bathroom were further down the back, without a roof. Humble as it was, for our family it was like a blessed honeycomb after our year's separation in Phnom Penh.

My uncle Hoa stayed with us for three months. It did not seem that he was jobless; but he was not doing regular work. He would leave home and return at unusual times. Sometimes he did not come home for a week or so. He did not bother my parents for his personal needs; instead, he contributed a regular amount of money as the rent of his room. We could not understand my uncle's life.

I still recall my childhood impression of him as a gentle, dashing young man. He was only about 160 centimeters tall, was thin with a rather large forehead and had dark shining eyes hidden under prominent eyebrows. His long black hair, parted far to the left side, made the other side appear longer and caused the hair to hang partly over his right eye. But he always looked very smart in his white shirt, black trousers, black shoes and white socks, with a little perfume lingering around him. He had the image of a Western film star in the nineteen-fifties. He was quiet, but could become animated and warm when he talked to someone he liked.

One day my mother saw him dressed nicely just before leaving home, but his shirt was too long and baggy.

'Why wasn't it made smaller to fit you?' my mother said.

'Do I look funny, sister?' my uncle warmly asked. 'This was given to me by a friend. I must wear it as it is.'

'But I can make it smaller for you. It just doesn't look right!' my mother insisted.

'Thanks, sister. But I don't care. The roomier it is, the easier for me to breathe!' And he laughed. He then changed the conversation to another subject.

To the left at the street light, please!' My father raised his voice to make sure the truck driver heard him.

The truck, big and heavy like a monster, slowly crawled into a long narrow road off the main street into an area interlaced with hundreds of houses, brick and timber, large and small, where my uncle used to live with his wife and his in-laws.

This was Phu Nhuan, a typical Saigon suburb. Thousands of people lived in this crowded tangled area. Those who happened to be born there and grew up in one of the houses in this kind of area did not understand why the area was like it was. Each house was built the shape of its own piece of land — large or small, square or triangle, wide or narrow. All were interwoven in such a way that, if seen from the air, they would look like a huge cobweb of a monster spider.

The truck stopped. A small kerosene light was hurriedly brought to the front room after much insistent knocking by the police. A young woman, half asleep, answered.

'Monsieur Hoa? We want him immediately. He's under arrest!' the French sûreté barked.

'But. . . my husband is not here!' Buu Lan answered, frightened and astonished. Within a minute, the whole family appeared in the front room.

The father-in-law, aged about fifty, was trembling. 'May I ask why my son-in-law is under arrest?'

'Search the house immediately!' the French sûreté ordered angrily without bothering to answer the old man.

Quickly the two Vietnamese police rushed into the house to the bedroom first, forced up the mosquito nets with their guns, searched under the beds and in the wardrobe; then they hurried to the kitchen, bathroom, toilet and a small extra upstairs room. Nothing seemed suspicious. My uncle was certainly not there.

'Viet minh! That's what he is! Where's he gone, eh?' the French angrily shouted into Buu Lan's face. The family was stunned. They stared at each other in shock.

'Oh no! I thought he was only a playboy sponging on family and friends,' the mother-in-law uttered, then continued, 'Please kindly reconsider. He is such a useless man! He would not dare to do that sort of thing.'

But the French did not understand a word from her as she spoke in Vietnamese. 'Hmm! Clever!' said the officer, tight-ening his lips.

Suddenly he turned to my father and grumbled, 'That's clever! By the time we know the right place, he's already gone beyond our reach.'

In the gloomy light of the house and over the shoulders of the French sûreté, the sister-in-law caught sight of my father who was standing outside on the veranda. She was nonplussed.

'I'll explain it to you later, sister!' With this, my father was forced to turn round by the two Vietnamese security police. They pushed him back onto the truck. And again in the middle of the night, my father was brought back home.

*　　　*　　　*

I remember my father telling us of his early life.

After the death of his widowed mother, life became so hard that my father, his three brothers and an older sister, who were all in their teens, were forced to find their own support and go their separate ways. They left a young sister and brother in the care of a relative who was a rice farmer.

Their hardships meant they did not see each other for almost two years. My father recalled how one day, from a remote area close to the South China Sea where he had been working as a river trading man learning the business from a kind old man, he was shocked to learn that Kim, his twelve-year-old sister, was being exploited by her landowning employer.

My father was tearful as he recalled the day he quit his job to go back to Vinh Kim village in My Tho province to rescue his small sister. From the day they all gathered around the grave to pay their last tribute to their mother, he felt deeply how miserable life is for an orphan. Their lives from that moment were like dust being blown by the wind.

My father made a secret visit to see Kim.

'Brother, I can't go with you! Uncle and his wife did not have enough rice to pay their debt from last year. That's why they put me here!' she said.

My father looked at his small sister, and the huge five-apartment house located in the middle of the fifty acre rice plot with hundreds of farmers and peasants working on it. Her sharp-featured face and neglected long thin hair dangling about her pale face made her look like a skeleton. He knew she could never be released from this debt.

'My poor little thing! You must listen to me, or the souls of our dear parents will never be at rest. You must leave this place. I'll look after you!'

'But how, brother?' The little girl peered into her brother's eyes. 'You don't have enough money to buy me out, do you?'

'I'll kidnap you! I'm going to!' Kim was startled by her brother's wild idea. It was too much for her to comprehend. She silently hoped that the spirit of her parents would protect her brother whatever he was going to do.

Kim slept in the rice store. So my father asked her to leave the door unlocked and to stay awake waiting for him. Then my father wandered aimlessly around a local market place until evening and secretly came back to the landowner's property. He hid in a huge haystack. At midnight he went to the storeroom where Kim was waiting for him. It was close to harvest time; the rice plants grew thick and tall. My father took his sister's hand and both forced their way through the rice fields. In the dark they heard sounds of dogs and people chasing them.

Hoa also left the farm that day. Though it was always difficult, both he and Kim survived a frugal childhood with their brothers.

My uncle Hoa was about fourteen when his brother Luong introduced him to his first job.

Luong had a job as a housekeeper for a group of four men who were working in Saigon city. These men worked in an office and spoke French fluently. Whether single or married, they were living here by themselves. As housekeeper, Luong's job covered everything — shopping, cooking, washing, ironing and cleaning. He did the job well.

One day, one middle-aged man moved out of the group house and stayed by himself in a small house nearby. He asked Luong to engage someone to work for him at home; someone who 'is nice and good just like you', he said. Luong thought of his brother Hoa, though he realised that Hoa was a little too young for this kind of responsibility.

During this time, both my father's and mother's families became Christians. They were some of the earliest members of the Evangelical Church in Vietnam. My parents met each other in Saigon, became engaged and

married shortly after. Sponsored by an American missionary couple, my parents completed a four-year course of
Bible theology. They were assigned to a small church not
far from Saigon city.

My father had come from a rather interesting religious
background. He was from Caodaism, a religious sect
which is considered a synthesis of Buddhism, Con-
fucianism-Taoism and Christianity. It includes Jesus Christ,
Buddha, Joan of Arc and Charlie Chaplin. The symbol of
worship of the Cao Dai (meaning 'High Tower' or 'Super
Power') is 'One centred eye' which is supposed to see
everything. This religion was militaristic and political. Its
members were protected by their own army.

My father did not recall in detail how his parents
became followers of this unusual religion rather than the
traditional Buddhism practiced throughout the country.
But he believed it must have been due to the tremendous
pressure felt by lower class people under the French. The
people needed something tangible rather than just a
mysterious theory — a kind of protection for themselves.

My mother, on the other hand, was from a strong
Catholic background. When her father chose to turn to the
Evangelical Church, his relatives and friends bitterly mocked him as being tempted by an 'American religion' with a
very shallow doctrine. My mother and her family were cast
out by their original Catholic Church, by relatives and
friends, and were even expelled from their original diocese.

My uncle Hoa lived with my parents and worked for
the middle-aged man from the other group. Though very
quiet, he was an intelligent and energetic teenager. He had
creative skills. He enjoyed learning new recipes from my
mother. He seemed, at this stage, very content with what
he was doing. He had one peculiar habit. Wherever he
was, Hoa always had in his shirt pocket a small notebook,

greasy and crumpled. He would take it out, look in it for a while and, while putting the notebook back in his pocket, would mumble something. Then he repeated the whole thing again and again.

'What are you doing, Hoa? You're not mad, are you?' my mother asked impatiently.

'No, for sure, sister!' He smiled as he swung himself like an innocent little boy in the hammock hung in the kitchen. 'I'll tell you if I've gone mad, sister!'

My mother burst into laughter. She did not understand what my young uncle was doing.

That was the time Hoa began learning French from the middle-aged man for whom he had been working for almost two years. This man secretly revealed information about the Viet minh anti-French movement and implanted in him the idea of a life which was more meaningful, more adventurous and more victorious than the life of a slave under the French.

'We need young people like you. You'll help to liberate our people. Nothing is better than independence and freedom!' the man explained to my uncle. 'It needs not only intelligence but also patience, both of which I've seen in you. Yes, this land is ours, not theirs, not even a tiny bit!' He continued talking confidently, totally convinced it would be only a matter of a few years. 'First, you've got to learn to speak French, which I'll teach you. I'm sure you can learn it easily.'

This man was right. Within two years, Hoa had learnt to speak French fluently. Nobody would have believed that he who used to be an orphan and had had no chance to complete his basic education would have been able to learn such a difficult language in such a short time. At the same time, he had been trained as a Viet minh secret agent to work in south Vietnam.

Amazingly, Hoa had kept this secret to himself, even from our family, close relatives and friends.

The years passed quickly. Everybody from my father's family had grown up, married and had their own families. They all lived in the same area. Each family's home was only a short walk from the others, except for Hoa who had been living with his wife at his parents-in-law's home in another inner Saigon district.

Secretly Hoa had taken over the middle-aged man's Viet minh responsibilities. He was a liaison officer, working undercover to find out how much the central sûreté knew about the Viet minh's activities, their strategy of defence and their military capability. Then he distributed the information to the local resistance forces for action against the French. His job with the French was as a sûreté working at the central security office. Both the French and the Vietnamese collaborators trusted him as a friend, enjoyed his company and admired his ability.

Nguyen Van Hao Building in Boulevard Gallieni, later Tran Hung Dao Street, was a prestigious three-storey structure, constructed by the French close to the heart of the city. The Nguyen Van Hao national music theatre occupied the first two floors. On the third floor were a number of apartments, mostly rented by the French. One of them was my uncle Hoa's permanent residence for many years, but none of us knew it until much later.

During these years, Hoa lived a life of pleasure, and appeared useless to his family and friends. While working for the French he betrayed them out of a willingness to sacrifice his life for the sake of the Viet minh anti-French movement. As time went on, Hoa's task became more difficult. The more the resistance attacks increased, the more the French became suspicious about the Vietnamese. Hoa sensed he was in danger.

He left his apartment without taking anything It was then that he pleaded with my parents to stay with them on the false grounds, mentioned earlier, that he could not get on with his in-laws. His sudden departure was because he knew the order by the French sûreté to capture him was about to be issued. None of his relatives or friends knew exactly where he was, though they knew he had fled to *Chien Khu*, the fighting zone, to escape the French.

In those days southern Vietnamese invested the word 'fight' with deep meaning. It was for peace and justice in their own country which had been cruelly destroyed by the colonial French. *Chien Khu* had become a secret world where the young people gathered voluntarily and were trained to become fighters against the French. It could be any remote area far from habitation where people could easily avoid the French and express their nationalist aspirations.

One hot evening, my family had just finished dinner and were gathered in the front room. My father was sitting at one end of a large table, set in the middle of the room, quietly reading his Bible to seek inspiration for his next sermon. Scattered around him were reference books. At the other end, my sister Tuyet and I were doing our school-work, while my mother was still busy with my younger sisters and brother around the house.

The door of the front room was half closed. Tuyet suddenly yelled, staring at the door, 'Papa, it's uncle Hoa! Uncle, where have you been? We missed you!' Tuyet burst out.

Hoa's absence for more than a year made my sisters and me think that he and my parents would never be willing to make up. At that time we did not know the truth behind his disappearance.

'Oh God! Such a long time! Come right inside, Hoa!'

my mother cried, rushing to the door. Overtaken by surprise, she did not greet him properly. She urged Hoa to come to the next room immediately. My father followed them after asking my sister and me to stay where we were.

'Try to do your homework, my dear,' my father said.

Hoa passed our table with a smile. He touched a finger on his lips to make a sign for my sister and me to keep silent.

Because of the heat, most people would sit in front of their house to get some breeze. 'Did anybody see you when you came in?' my mother asked with a worried look.

'Everything is all right now, sister!' Hoa said. 'I come to say hello to you and family; and to say sorry for what I did to you before.'

'Where have you been, Hoa? We were concerned for you. The sûreté has been watching me for any hint about where you are,' my father said anxiously.

'I'm sorry, brother. I didn't mean to bother you.' Hoa looked around to make sure there was nobody else except the family. 'Don't worry, brother. I understand you, and your position with the church. I wouldn't bother you like I did last time. It was such an unfortunate situation.'

My mother held her breath and stared at Hoa. 'You really mean you've been working for them? And you are still?'

Hoa lowered his voice, firmly and confidently. 'I've changed my image. I'm a normal, hard-working person. I've also changed my name on my identification card to Ho To Tam. The sûreté can't trace my identity, I'm sure.'

Hoa had two small children under ten years old. The name 'To' was that of his daughter, and 'Tam', his son. 'Ho' was the surname of Ho Chi Minh. Hoa proudly explained that his new name indicated his love for his children, and his admiration for the person whom the southern Vietnamese regarded as the great hero of national liberation.

'What exactly are you doing now, Hoa? Have you ever thought of your wife and children?' my father asked.

Hoa did not answer him. He stood up and shook my father's hand firmly. 'You asked what I've been doing? I'm working to save our country. Someone must do something, or nothing can ever be done. Brother, I appreciate your concern for me. But I must go on with my task. You must keep everything secret.'

My mother was overwhelmed by what she was seeing of Hoa. The picture in her mind of a little boy, shy and gentle, was being transformed to that of a strong man of mystery. She felt she had lost a brother and a past full of closeness and understanding.

'Goodbye, sister! Goodbye, brother!' Hoa said as he paused at the doorstep.

'May God keep you in his hands, my brother!' said my mother, and sobbed.

Hoa was one of those who organised the finances of the *Chien Khu*. His area of responsibility was Cholon, the Chinatown district of Saigon. His first job was to collect the weapons stolen from the French by his contacts; the second was to collect money, in cash, from the Chinese *thuong gia*, businessmen, in Cholon. Hoa then found a way to transport what he had to the jungles for the use of the Viet minh.

Hoa intimidated the Cholon businessmen who would hand him a large amount of money any time he came. If they didn't, some kind of tragedy would happen to them. They bought their safety by providing him with money secretly and regularly. What kind of threats did Hoa use that made the Chinese scared of him? We never knew.

It had been some time since my parents last saw my uncle Hoa. Hoa's secret was still kept safe from my father's other brothers and sisters. To everybody, he was a businessman travelling from the city to the provinces. One December evening at about 7.00 p.m., Hoa suddenly appeared at his eldest sister's home. The sister and her family were happy to see him.

'Have you been home yet, Hoa?' his sister asked.

'Not yet, sister. I'm just back from the province. First, I've got to see a friend who's living near here. So I thought I'd drop in to say hello to you. Then I'll go home. Everything's all right with you, sister?'

'Fine. Everything's fine,' the sister answered happily.

'Sister, can I leave my briefcase here? I'll come back and get it around nine o'clock tonight if it's all right with you,' Hoa asked in an unemotional voice.

There was nothing to cause the eldest sister worry. A briefcase was a normal possession for a traveller. There was perhaps a pair of pyjamas, a towel, or a toothbrush inside. That was what she thought. And Hoa left.

He did not come back at nine o'clock as he had said. Not even during the next few days! His eldest sister had a feeling that something was really wrong. She opened the briefcase and almost choked. Money! Stacks of money jammed under a large old bath towel. Never in her life had she seen such a large amount of money. It looked like a fortune.

The eldest sister realised this was not a joke. She ran to tell my parents. 'Just leave it as it is!' my father said in a shaken voice. 'Put it in the most unlikely spot in the house and wait for him. I don't know what else to suggest to you.'

'But I'll throw it down the toilet, if I hear there could be a random check!' his sister said in a terrified voice.

This was one of the few times when the secret of those trips leaked out and Hoa was on the 'escape route' from the French security forces, carrying the extortion money taken from the Chinese businessmen.

Another time Hoa was in the same predicament. He knew he could not lie to his eldest sister if he wanted help. He told her frankly, 'All the expensive guns are in there, sister. Please help! Don't destroy them if you don't have to.'

The sister felt she would faint. She could not bear what she called the 'mental breakdown game' played by her young brother. She attacked him and vowed never to let him inside her house again.

In fact Hoa had been secretly followed by the French central security for many months. He was on the edge of life and death. But it was too late to draw back from what he had been doing.

What happened next was a nightmare to the family.

My father was called in to the Catinat central security office to receive his brother Hoa who had just been granted a reprieve from the death sentence issued by the sûreté after they had captured him a few months previously.

When Hoa came out of prison, he looked like a battered bird. His head was shaven, swollen with scratches and bruised: he had been the target of sûreté interrogations.

Hoa recalled the tortures he had suffered. The Catinat sûreté made him stand on a wooden base close to a large tank full of water. His arms were tied behind his back. His head was pushed down into the water. Then two Vietnamese police were ordered to beat both sides of the tank with a huge rope. At other times, while he stood in the same place and position, an electric shock was passed through the water, and his whole body sprang backwards, leaving him unconscious for hours. Another torture was to lay him facing upwards on a base with his arms tied and his head back; then a whole bottle of salty *nuoc mam*, fish sauce, was poured over his face and nostrils until he choked and fought for air like a raging cat.

My father could not stop thinking of how things had turned out for his brother. It was not at all the way he had prayed and hoped.

In response to my father's request, a missionary had dialled the telephone number in front of her eyes. After introducing herself to the person at the other end, the missionary realised that she had made a mistake! She was not speaking to the prison superintendent with whom she wanted to arrange a time of prayer with my uncle Hoa before the execution; it was the chief of the Bureau de Sûreté! The missionary had dialled the wrong number! A short unexpected conversation to the head of sûreté and my uncle Hoa's execution was transformed to a pardon. To the missionary and my parents it was an amazing and merciful thing!

However, Hoa disappeared into the jungles again. The only thought my father had was that Hoa was stuck too fast in the mud; he could no longer draw himself back.

One day in mid-1951 a stranger — a woman — appeared at my father's eldest sister's with a message that my uncle Hoa, who was in a *Chien Khu* near Saigon, had been very sick and was in a critical condition. He needed proper treatment and intensive care from his family.

The woman had contacted Hoa's wife who was still living with her own parents. Though the in-laws felt sorry for him, they refused to receive him back home because they were frightened of being linked with the Viet minh. After a serious talk with my father and the other brothers, my uncle Hoa was secretly brought to his eldest sister's home. For three months, Hoa was cared for by the entire family of his sister and brothers. His wife secretly came over from her home to take care of him during the daytime. He was suffering from malaria and dysentery.

Hoa could not be taken to hospital for the right treatment. A respected Chinese medicine man who belonged to one of the churches in the city was asked by my father to treat Hoa. Though skilled, kindly and willing, nothing much he could do by using herbs helped. My uncle Hoa was in a semi-coma and his jaw locked. Since he had been brought home, all he could do was nod slightly in response to simple requests.

One night after midnight, my father was sitting next to Hoa's bed half asleep. It was his turn to watch his brother until early morning.

'Brother! Brother!' My father woke up, startled. It was Hoa calling. My father stared at his brother thinking he was in a dream. 'Brother! I want to speak to you!' Hoa said clearly. His eyes looked straight up into the immense silence of the house.

'Are you all right, brother? Are you really awake?' My father was so excited! 'Wake up, everybody!' he called to the family softly but excitedly. 'Hoa is getting better. He's speaking now!'

'No, brother. I don't want the rest of the family,' Hoa said calmly.

'Your wife is here. Do you want to talk to her?' my father asked.

'No, brother,' Hoa answered. 'I only want to talk to you. I'll be going soon forever. You're the only one I've trusted. Please take this message carefully and pass it on to my "comrade leader".' Then Hoa began speaking in French. He wanted to avoid other members of the family listening to what he said. He told my father that someone would make contact about the work he had been doing.

*   *   *

I recall the day when our entire family attended my uncle Hoa's funeral. We were in shock when we met the guests — Hoa's Viet minh comrades and his Vietnamese sûreté friends. Behind their closed faces they all tried to conceal their secrets from each other, but there was unstated anger at French inhumanity — against an innocent person or a patriot, depending on your point of view.

As a teenager I often thought of the kind of value system the French, as a cultured people, presented. What kind of justice and Christianity did they try to convey to the Vietnamese people? A deep resentment was sparked among many of the young. They swore to stand together and fight until justice could be seen in their land.

5

The ragged toy:
1954 – 1963

I SAT ON THE ROUGH WOODEN BENCH in a tiny, over-crowded classroom, trying hard to concentrate on the French literature lesson. 'The eighteenth century was the century during which the most romantic literature was produced in France.' The teacher recited the beginning of a poem. 'Souvent sur la montagne, à l'ombre du vieux chêne.'

I suddenly felt sick of this ridiculous unreality. 'Please stop, teacher!' I angrily whispered to my classmate. 'I don't want to hear it! It's not that romantic! I'm not sitting on the mountain under the shade of an old oak tree at all! I'm here suffocating inside a "warehouse turned into a school". It's hot, dark and stuffy! Look what the colonialists and imperialists have left to us — not the beauty described in their literature. They're savages!'

The ceiling fan only stirred up the steamy air in the classroom, draining the minds of those of us who had tried hard to absorb the unrealistic meaning of their lesson. The last hour of a school day — from eleven to twelve in the morning — was always too suffocating to be constructive.

Suddenly the school courier appeared in our class. He handed an office message to the teacher. 'Tran Minh Tam! Please pay your school fees or I'll have to ban you from class!' The teacher focussed on a student sitting at the back of the room. A vaguely guilty feeling pervaded the classroom. 'Did you hear me, Tam?' The teacher repeated his request and ordered the student to leave the room immediately.

'What the hell do you think you're doing, teacher?' Tam burst out. 'How much have you already ripped us off? Look at the facilities you've provided! You have no pity on the poor, yet you have more than enough!'

'Go to the office! I'll not tolerate that sort of thing!' The teacher was trembling with anger.

'Shame on you, teacher!' Tam mumbled angrily. He stood up, threw his long legs over his desk and squeezed between rows in order to leave class. Don't say you're teaching us dissertation morale when you have no morals!' 'Dissertation morale' was a kind of long essay done by students to help them develop life values.

'Shut up, young man! Get out of my sight!'

We all felt sorry for what had happened to our classmate who was a few days late in paying his monthly school fees because of his family's financial problems.

Our teacher of French literature was one of the board members of a private high school which my eldest sister and I attended. These board members were educated in French and came originally from Hanoi, fleeing to the south soon after the 1954 Geneva Accords were signed.

This was the second private high school the two of us had attended. A few months earlier when we were at our previous school, one member of the school board was accused by the police of being a Viet minh secret agent. The principal and some of our teachers quickly disappeared after this news broke out. We did not know whether they had run away for fear of being arrested or whether they were actually arrested. The school was closed by the authorities then and the students left. It had been difficult to find another school in the middle of the school year.

The political situation in Vietnam was chaotic during the important years of my schooling. The 1954 Geneva Agreement between the French and Viet minh had been signed. Vietnam had a different but not better political structure, a disunited country in which the seeds of the tragic Vietnam war were sown. It revealed the previously hidden goal of the Vietnamese communists whose leader for a long time had posed as a great patriot, and had used the Vietminh nation-alists to fight against the French for his own ambition. The historic exodus of almost a million north Vietnamese to the south proved what communism was like.

Saigon was my home town, the city which was named by the French *Hon Ngoc Vien Dong*, 'the Gem of the Far East'. It had many sources of richness and abundance. Despite this, there were only two small public high schools established in the whole city for those who could not afford private education. These same schools were also open to receive all southern students who had finished their primary schooling in provinces or smaller towns and wished to continue their education in this more advantaged city.

A restrictive entrance examination was organised by the administrators every academic year to select the students who could best be moulded to the colonial pattern. Besides these two schools, there were two colleges reserved for Saigon citizens who had money and power, Lycée Jean Jacques Rousseau and Lycée Chasseloup Laubat. Consequently, thousands were not given the chance of continuing their education. Later, a small number of private schools were established by business people, but these often exploited the poor.

Ngo Dinh Diem became the first president of

newly-independent Vietnam. It was 1955. Diem was unknown to the majority of Vietnamese when he returned from
the USA to take up his presidency. Later people came to know
that he and his family had served as high level officials under
the previous Nguyen royal dynasty. He was single, in his
mid-fifties, with a strong Catholic background and a reputation of having lived his life like a priest.

At first I was delighted for my country with the thought
that a religious man 'without his own family' would be a
perfect leader. He would lead his country with devotion
and he would not fall into the trap of self-indulgence or
nepotism and neglect what a leader should do for his
country.

However, during the eight years under his government,
the republic was led into administrative chaos and was torn
apart by power struggles. National religious sects such as
Binh Xuyen, Cao Dai and Hoa Hao emerged with their
own armies to oppose the government. This led to
widespread violence.

Our family was caught up in a fierce fight that raged
for four days between the Binh Xuyen religious sect and
the government troops. The day after my father took the
risk of evacuating our family to another area, our home was
hit by shell fire and destroyed, together with many others.
My family had to move to a rural area temporarily, about
thirty kilometres away from my school. The bicycle was
the only means of transport for me and my sister to go to
school every day. We felt so low physically and spiritually
and had totally lost the will to work at school.

During Diem's regime, his family gained such power
that people named this period 'Diem's Dynasty'. Some
blame Diem because he lacked the balance in his life of a
woman of his own. He was considered weak and lacked
confidence in his own leadership. People thought perhaps

this was the reason why Diem was used by the USA to lead Vietnam. Others blamed him for being 'too religious', an attitude, they said, which never suits a country's leadership.

There was total confusion. The Vietnamese communist terrorists during this time would infiltrate wherever they could in the south in various guises with the purpose of causing sabotage. Their aim was to create a secret network to prepare for their invasion of the south. During Diem's regime they disguised themselves as Buddhists. The pure Buddhists were true to their religion and were deeply hurt by Diem's policies which they saw as anti-Buddhist.

Thich Quang Duc, a devout Saigon Buddhist monk, protested against Diem by immolating himself in the middle of a busy Saigon street. This event shocked the world, but provided little help in explaining the political tangle in Vietnam during this time. In truth Diem was not wrong in having continual random checks of Buddhist temples and dioceses to identify Viet Cong who falsely wore the monk's robes; but on many occasions Diem's forces abused their power and alienated many people.

On the other hand, Madame Nhu, Diem's sister-in-law, used this situation to her own benefit. Using Diem's policies and exercising her powerful influence as the 'Grand Dame' of Vietnam in place of the President's wife, she had the Buddhists tortured, and praised the Catholics — both Diem's and her family were Catholics — to get their support for enhancing her power.

In late 1959 my parents moved to the Mekong delta region to take up new church responsibilities. I finished my high school and decided to join them. Then I joined the public service, working in the provincial office.

By this time the word 'Viet minh' had disappeared from the vocabulary of common people. Diem's government had been organising the nationwide *to cong*, 'denouncing communists' campaign, to educate people about the hypocrisy of Ho Chi Minh — a communist posing as a nationalist — whose cunning scheme was to dye the south red. The word 'Viet Cong', literally 'Vietnamese communist', was used consistently in public speeches, literature and in the press with derogatory overtones. From cities to provinces to the most remote areas, people sensed the pressure to involve themselves in this campaign. It was important to be regarded as a loyal citizen, especially for people in the public service.

One day my office manager asked me to see him in his office. 'Phuong,' he said, 'I think you should take part in the *to cong* monthly campaign, and also join the *Phu Nu Ban Quan Su*, Women's Army Reserve.

At this stage I was naive on these political issues. 'I'm sorry. I can't do that sort of thing, Uncle. (Uncle was a term of respect to a man of my father's age.) I'm ignorant of politics. I'm also hopeless in physical exercises!'

The manager gave me a warning look. 'This is not my invitation. It's the deputy provincial chief's request. And remember, joining the Women's Army Reserve is every young woman's responsibility!'

'But what am I going to do at these campaigns?' I tried to hide my depression and annoyance.

'It's important to take part in both. But for the *to cong*, all you have to do is to join the music program at interval. Leave other things to the people in charge. You sing very well, don't you?'

The manager smiled at me when he mentioned that everybody in this small town had heard the church's weekly broadcasting program in which I normally took part in the solo singing. Everybody liked my singing. He joked that he felt honoured to be my boss — but I could see that it would be better not to let him down.

There was no doubt in my family, in the churches and amongst our friends about my natural gift of singing; however, in my young days I always believed that the church was too ordinary a place to suit my high profile ambitions. I sang in the church because I loved my parents and wanted to please them; but privately I planned to find a way which would give me greater recognition. However, this kind of pressure on my singing made me feel as though my precious youth and my gift were being belittled. I was angry at myself for falling into this situation; and I felt a deep bitterness.

The *to cong* campaign, however, did not help people to understand about the communists. It only increased people's anxiety at being under constant pressure.

Later, together with other young women from the public service and public schools, I had to learn how to use guns of different types. Sometimes we were transported to the field for shooting practice. I remember Trinh, one of the teachers from the provincial high school and a fragile young woman, lying flat on her stomach behind a small heap of earth with a heavy gun in her hands pretending to ambush Viet Cong. An American military man was always there at the shooting practices as an adviser.

After loading the gun, Trinh aimed it at the target and nervously pressed the trigger. Within a second, many bullets were coughed out of the gun raucously and ceaselessly without her being aware of what had happened. Trinh dropped the gun in shock. She burst into tears like a little child. She actually forgot all that the American had explained. With this type of gun, Trinh had to press the trigger sensitively; otherwise it would happen like it had a minute before. I remember how nervous I was at the shooting practices. I always got a 'C' mark on the list and my office manager teased me.

The shooting practice — and other public services — was a result of pressure from Madame Nhu. One morning after coming back from the shooting field, the manager asked me, 'Is tomorrow your turn to work at *Quan Com Xa Hoi*, "Eating House for the Poor"?'

'Yes,' I said.

He looked at my in-tray and sighed, 'Too much time for Madame! But you'd better. Otherwise neither you nor I will be safe!' When I told him what happened to the teacher at the shooting field, he shook his head with an air of depression: 'Truly, morale and virtue are being turned upside down in this country!'

The public eating house opened to the poor was another social activity for women directed by Diem's sister-in-law. Every woman working in the public service had to take turns to contribute a day of cooking and serving lunch and dinner at this eating shop where rice and food were supposedly provided free or at low price by the local administrative authority to help poor workers and labourers. The project was supposedly operated from a government budget; in practice most things came from the local public servants' own contribution as the result of pressure.

*   *   *

One day I visited Khue, one of my married sisters who had been living with her in-laws in a small province about fifty kilo-metres east of Saigon.

Her in-laws' rough timber home was one of hundreds built in an area that they had carved out of virgin forest. The government divided the land into many one acre blocks meas-ured equally alongside the main national road, and sold them to ordinary people at an affordable price. The bonus offer was that those who had the capacity to develop the area behind their property would own it themselves. This was one of the policies directed by Ngo Dinh Nhu, Diem's brother and also his adviser. Its stated reason was to help the rural population build a solid future. At the same time it meant that innocents could be more easily protected against Viet Cong terrorists.

Like everybody in the same area, my sister's in-laws bought the land, made their home on it and worked hard to cultivate it, hoping it would become a profitable family asset.

On the second day of my visit, at about 5.00 a.m., while it was still dark and quiet outside, I woke up feeling rested from a beautiful sleep and decided to make myself a cup of green tea. I went to the kitchen and was surprised. Almost everybody in the family was already there. They were all silent and looked extremely worried.

My sister quietly showed me a note, a crumpled piece of paper with handwriting on it. It read, 'The South Liberation Front requests your cooperation: 10 kgs of rice, 5 kgs of dried fish, 2 kgs of salt, and as many antibiotics as you can get. Collection time: 2.00 a.m. tomorrow. Venue: your back door. No assistance needed. Important: your immediate response and top secrecy are your safety!' My sister's mother-in-law had found the note pushed through the front door sill early that morning.

It appeared like a joke, but indeed was true and deadly. Later that morning, just like the other neighbours who had received the same secret note, Khue's mother-in-law went to the market and bought everything as instructed without saying why. She carefully waited until about 1.45 a.m., the supposedly most difficult time for the government night security guards to stay awake and put a bamboo basket filled with the secret contribution outside the back door. She closed the door and went to bed. In the morning all had disappeared.

One evening in July 1961, Khue, her husband and their two-year-old daughter suddenly appeared unexpectedly at the door of our parents' home. It was such a long way to travel from their home to our province if it was not for a good reason. This action was unexplained while we greeted each other. What was wrong? At last Khue sighed with relief when she learnt there was nothing wrong with us.

It was only the day before that my sister had been asked to mind the bush home for her mother-in-law while she went away to visit a relative and stayed overnight with that family. The following morning, her mother-in-law suddenly rushed home. She burst out crying before she had even stepped inside the house. 'Khue, you must go back to your father right away! He is dying and asking for all the children. Poor old man. He's such a kind man!' She wiped her tears and continued: 'I've just got the sudden news from our relative who arrived from Saigon.'

The mother-in-law urged my sister and her husband to try to catch the next bus to Saigon which would pass the town in half-an-hour. Then from Saigon they had to catch another bus to go to our parents' place without delay. 'Your father's waiting for you every minute!' the mother said anxiously.

Tearfully, Khue quickly packed up her things, and with her husband and their small daughter they left immediately for the city, then for father's province. Standing next to the bus before departure, the mother whispered to her son, 'Stay with your wife as long as you can. I'll explain to your boss.'

A week later, Khue and her husband received a letter from the mother posted from Saigon. It said, 'I made up the reason for you to leave our home without hesitation and without being suspected. Don't go back home! The

South Liberation Front has secretly requested you to join their local force immediately to fight against *De quoc My*, American Imperialists. Please ask your parents to forgive me for using that terrible reason! Also, please ask them to help you in settling in Saigon permanently. I'll see you whenever I can.'

Later many bombs were dropped by the government forces in that rural province in order to destroy the Viet Cong stronghold. Khue's mother-in-law was killed instantly after a bomb exploded right in front of the trench built outside her home. She was running from her house to her hiding place. An open Bible half-burnt and a pair of reading glasses were found the next day still lying on the table in her home.

*   *   *

In November 1963, Diem was overthrown by a military coup. Tragically Diem and his brother Nhu were assassinated after being expelled by those army generals who used to be their loyal subjects. The fatal coup was organised with the cooperation of most of the high level military officers from Diem's government. They could no longer cope with the shameful weakness of their leader and the unbearable abuse of power by his sister-in-law!

Vietnam during this decade was like a ragged toy. It had been torn apart by invasions of Chinese, Japanese, French and by early Vietnamese communists. After this the country had been given to an older brother to mind. He was irresponsible, and the other naughty children in his family ambitiously fought to take the toy for their own pleasure. It was an idiotic senseless chapter in the country's history. Sadly, for better or for worse, the innocent people endured it all.

On the morning after the assassination of Diem and Nhu, I went to my office. Instead of a routine salute of the national flag before work, we were all confused and sat around in our office to wait for a new order from the provincial chief. Later, official word came that we were to work normally until a further message from the new military authority. The large portrait of Diem hanging in the centre of the office wall was quickly removed with the help of some staff.

I felt as if I was sitting in a theatre during the change of scenes of a play and wondered what was going to be in the next scene.

6

Innocent victims of war: 1964 – 1965

THE AMERICAN MAJOR, ONE OF THE TEACHERS at the evening English classes, grasped his crewcut hair in exasperation with both hands and stared at me. 'What? Working for Australians? You must be joking!'

I looked at the American in a bewildered fashion. 'Why? No, I'm serious. I'm going to sit for the English test. If I pass I'll work for the Australian surgical team. You've heard about them coming to this province soon, haven't you?'

'I'm sorry, Phuong!' He seemed very concerned for me. 'What kind of test are you going to have?'

'There'll be two. Written and oral,' I said.

'I must be honest with you, Phuong. Though you're one of my best students, I bet you won't understand a single word from the Australians at the oral test!'

'But they speak English, don't they?' I asked anxiously.

'Well yes, in a way they do!' The American laughed. 'But their accent! Yes, I mean the Australian accent. Terrible! It's terrible really!'

The American major felt he had caused me to be sad, so he gave me a soft smile and said, 'Even me, Phuong! Sometimes they drive me crazy, I must admit!'

I left my evening class and walked home. The thought of taking the English test still lingered in my mind. I asked myself how I would understand the Australian accent if the American teacher could not. I wondered what the accent would be like. I felt so worried!

My youth and dreams were passing swiftly. It had been two years now since I had moved to this province with my parents. As a young woman in my early twenties I had become bored living in my small town. Although my job was very busy and my income was adequate, I did not have anything to spend it on. The weekends were usually taken up with church activities.

Regret at having given up my studies somehow kept gnawing at me. I thought I should have stayed back in Saigon to pursue my career at any cost, rather than be wrapped up in the monotonous life of this sleepy town. This was not my wish; in fact coming to this province was contrary to my dreams and hopes. I felt lost, lonely and ill at ease among the local people, even of my own age. The more I tried to understand myself through the Bible, the more confused I became. I wished something spiritual could happen to me in a more practical way to help me understand the purpose of my life.

It was now only a few weeks before the English tests were to take place to recruit three people to work for the Australian surgical team. The administrative office was responsible for organising the examination in cooperation with USOM (United States Operations Mission). The oral test — the interview — would be taken by the Australian team; but that was only after the person had passed the written test.

I told my parents on impulse that I needed their prayers for this special day. I learnt that there were about thirty applicants, including local people and people from several neighbouring provinces. A rumour also spread around the administrative office where I was working that the deputy provincial chief's sister-in-law, a young Saigon woman, was one of the candidates. This depressed me badly because I was worried the rumour could possibly be a sign of pressure put on the responsible local authority to disadvantage the contestants so they would take the people they wanted. And it would be unfair for the others, including myself.

However, I wanted and hoped for a change, like some gentle breeze that had been expected in an endless summer. I felt anxious to go for the test, and to meet the Australian people, though I was worried about what the American major had warned me about. I was also concerned that the rumour about the young Saigon woman could possibly turn out to be true.

Then came the day of the exam. After one hour in the written test, the deputy provincial chief suddenly stepped into the room. Everybody tried to concentrate on their work, though we all realised that his presence in this room was strange. Technically he had nothing to do with this test.

He observed the room for a second; then addressed the supervisor who was standing by the desk watching us. 'Has anybody failed to show up? Good! Anyone from Saigon?' He did not mean to wait for the answers. 'Try hard to get the highest mark, everybody! Specially the local folks! Otherwise others will beat you with the same mark plus an extra qualification of some sort!' Then he smiled to the supervisor and walked out.

This attitude, though it was strange to the candidates, was seen often from this man by the local people and the administrative office staff. He was the second top authority in this province and considered he had a right to be involved in everything. Sitting on one of the back seats with the test half done, I murmured to myself, 'Oh dear!

I've already wasted my time. His sister-in-law has probably got the extra qualification he mentioned. I'm too small to fight against the bigger power!'

I perspired constantly. My mind went blank. My hands were shaking. The words on my test paper were dancing in front of my eyes. 'No, there's no hope, no hope!' I kept repeating. I packed up everything and raised my hand to show I was ready to go.

'Are you sure of everything?' The supervisor, surprised, asked. 'Another fifteen minutes to go. You can sit and check your test again, if you like!' I rushed to the desk and gave my test papers to her. I walked out to the great surprise of all the people in the room.

I should have gone back to my office to work normally if I was not going for the oral test. However that afternoon I stayed home tossing in deep despair. My parents had left the day before to go to a nearby province for a church regional convention. They were supposed to stay there for five days. Before they left I told them I would let them know if I passed the test.

At 2.30 p.m., about seven or eight people who had passed the written test were back at the office to be interviewed. I was not there! I had given up on passing the written test; I presumed I had failed and would not be required further.

At about 3.30 p.m. I was called back by the USOM office to meet the Australian team. I was stunned! I was told that the team was not satisfied after interviewing the other people. For the hospital work the team required two young women and a young man. However, the result was the other way round. Two young men were chosen as acceptable in English, but none of the women were.

'Is there anyone who did not come for the interview?' My test papers were chosen by the USOM office's assistant.

Unexpectedly I was called to come and meet the Australian team.

It was nothing like sitting for a job interview. It was friendly, not bureaucratic. The young Australian nurse, fresh in her white working uniform with her soft blue emblem from the Melbourne School of Nursing which shone on the left side of her collar, was petite (this surprised me a lot for a European woman!) and she was gentle. Next to her was the leader of the surgical team, Mr D.G. Macleish, the senior surgeon from Melbourne.

The interview began simply. 'Why do you want to work for us?'

'I enjoy speaking English and hope to have a chance to help the Vietnamese people.'

'Do you think you'd like to work in the hospital?'

'Yes, I think I would.'

'Is your father a church minister?'

'Yes, he is.'

And so the conversation went on.

Suddenly I asked myself in amusement, 'Where's the terrible accent gone? Am I talking to a real Australian? Because I can understand her every single word.'

'Are you able to start with us tomorrow at the hospital?'

I was astounded! Everything suddenly looked brighter and more beautiful. On the way to the post office, I drafted the cable to my parents: 'I have passed the test — what an amazing blessing!'

*   *   *

In late 1964, at the request of the new government whose Premier was Nguyen Van Thieu, the medical teams began to arrive from Vietnam's allies — the United States, Great Britain, Australia, New Zealand, Italy, Japan, South Korea and the Philippines. These teams worked in the south of Vietnam with the generous support of USOM (United States

Operations Mission). USOM also provided most of the medical equipment to the hospitals in south-ern Vietnam.

I still remember my feelings on the day the Australian surgical team was first welcomed to the province. I was still an 'outsider' to this provincial affair. I had not at that stage taken the English test. But nobody could miss a special event in a small town like mine. It was like a public holiday with all the province's VIPs and press people present at the provincial airfield.

National and Australian flags fluttered in the breeze along the main street leading to the provincial reception. Sparkling in their traditional white *ao dai* (the national dress and also schoolgirl uniform) were the beautiful high school girls who placed their garlands of fresh flowers around the necks of the Australian guests. Merry martial music sounded forth after the speeches. 'Long live Australian-Vietnamese friendship' said the provincial chief heartily. Excitement filled the air.

And now I was working with a team of seven from the Royal Melbourne Hospital. Their carefree manner, gentleness and sense of humour were in stark contrast to the hatred and violence of the ambitious war-makers. Their work later extended to the worst war-affected areas in the Mekong delta. The Royal Melbourne Hospital team opened the door for other Australian surgical teams from St Vincent's Hospital, Prince Henry's Hospital and one doctor from Fairfield Infectious Diseases Hospital. Each took turns to come to Vietnam during the war with the purpose of extending a helping hand to Vietnam. Their efforts and diligence were recognised by most Vietnamese as not only a diplomatic but also a humane response.

My everyday life was now woven into the activities of people who once did not know where Vietnam was and had had to look at the 'old school atlas' to find it, as Susan

Terry admitted.

As the impact of the war increased daily, I became obsessed with the hospital work. In the battlefields, people were fighting to kill; at the hospital the surgeons, doctors and nurses were fighting to save. Bombs and shells exploded at night; surgery was performed continuously the next day. Blood spilled and blood was given. A blood bank was born at this time to meet emergencies. The team members were among the first blood donors in this provincial hospital's history. Training the theatre nurses, teaching the use of medical equipment to the ward nurses, giving help and sharing difficulties with the Vietnamese hospital staff; all these were extra activities at the hospital, apart from their main mission.

At the hospital I knew for the first time what suffering and death were like. I matured in my thinking and came out of myself a little. Previously I had not found beauty and contentment in simpler things. But it was from this time that I learnt how to be content with what I had, to help my suffering people and to share the hard work with people of compassion.

*   *   *

I had watched the Australian team perform wonders on an unknown Vietnamese from the time he was handed over to the team by an American lieutenant and his fellow soldiers. From a muddy, bloody body he had become lively with the pleasant face of a young man in his early twenties. He looked secure and comfortable on a clean bed under a fresh sheet.

The surgeon told me he was shot twice in the back; the first bullet went through his right lung to his chest and the second stayed in the lung until the surgery was done. He was lucky to escape death after many hours of bleeding.

When he was first brought in, this young man was just

another wounded soldier. He was not unconscious but was too sick to be aware of things that were happening around him. His face was contorted with constant pain. In a weak, husky voice he asked continually for a little water. His military khaki clothes were caked with mud, dry and hard, like a kind of false cladding which broke piece by piece very time he moved.

Looking at him, I believed that he symbolised another 'fight for peace' somewhere on the battlefield and that he was probably one of those who were admired by civilians as heroes, the people who sacrifice their lives for the sake of peace in their homeland. Unfortunately, I thought, there were far more of those people than one could count on one's fingers; therefore their suffering or even death had become no more than just the fall of a withered leaf.

Then I watched the Vietnamese nurse prepare the patient to have his urgent surgery. She showed no emotion on her face. Was she a hard person herself? I did not think so, as she had chosen this job of compassion. Had she become hardened by hospital life and the constant suffering? Did she try to cope by not showing her emotions while on the job, because it would have become too much to bear?

Whatever they speculated about this patient, the Australian doctors and nurses saw him as a sick person in a critical condition. He needed their help and care to save his life. They were struggling every minute for him, no matter what his background was.

Nonetheless the young man, in the government's eyes, was a suspected Vietcong. Though he had been under intensive care from the doctors and nurses, his feet were bound to the bed with iron chains and he was guarded by an armed security officer outside the room.

The young American, a lieutenant, knew nothing more

about this man either. What he had done was a compassionate action by one person to another in need. He rescued him as he lay half dead in the mud on the river bank. While it was not easy, he was sure most of his American fellows would have done the same in the same situation.

The lieutenant related how he had found the man. It was about noon. The sun shone brightly over the vast ricefields along the side of the road. The military jeep had just covered the most rugged part of the national road; yet the American lieutenant still made sure he did not mistakenly turn off into the most dangerous part of this area. According to the military operations map, this turning point led straight to Tri Ton, a district belonging to Chau Doc province, a Vietcong stronghold. Any one of the district inhabitants could be a government supporter, or a guerilla, or be pressured by either side. Travelling mistakenly into this area meant meeting deadly danger.

At least they knew, after bypassing that turn-off, they were now in a safe area. The young American and his fellow soldiers stopped their jeep to find a rest spot. They walked just a little way into the scrub near the river. Suddenly, like being hit by an electric shock, they all reached for their rifles. Something was moving in the water! A person! Yes, a man! His body was half sunk in the mud.

With rifle in hand, the lieutenant moved closer, staring at him. Within a moment the man was pulled out of the mud and laid on the floor at the back of their jeep. The American soldiers then hurriedly continued their journey, carrying with them the unknown passenger.

Finally, they saw the street lights of the provincial town. And when the big cross painted in red in the middle of the hospital gate broke into two to let the dusty worn-out jeep in, everybody felt at peace. At least the hospital was here and not any further. They left the wounded man in the hands of the Australians.

'Please help me, miss! I'm not a Vietcong! I'm certainly not a VC!'

Standing next to Susan, I was supposed to interpret every word from the patient. My lips were sealed because I was confused. Where was the truth?

The wound from his back healed rapidly. Sometimes he gave a pleasant smile after receiving help from the doctors or nurses. I saw in him no difference to other civilians or soldiers. But the security guard was still outside, waiting for his recovery to take him away to some kind of punishment if he was indeed a Viet Cong.

The next day, Susan was changing his dressing. I was also there. The patient looked much better physically. He was calm, but the sadness on his face was obvious. 'Miss! Has anyone been looking for me?' he asked.

'No, nobody,' I said. 'Who are you expecting, may I ask?' The young man hesitated. I did not want to force him to answer me; but I was anxious to know more about what he had asked. 'What can I do for you if I happen to see someone?' I insisted. Again he did not respond to my question. I looked at him for a while and knew something was on his mind and he had to let it go.

'She is my fiancée. She is very attractive and lives in Tri Ton district. We love each other and had planned to get married soon. Then I received a warning secretly. I had to let her go to someone else; otherwise my life would be in danger!

'I was concerned for myself and my fiancée after receiving that warning, but did not believe in giving in to such a violent threat. Then on that fateful evening, I was sitting with her on the ricefield dam, planning our future. All of a sudden bullets came from somewhere in the bush and struck me in the back. To protect himself, my attacker made up the false accusation of my being a Viet Cong and he wanted to kill me to get my fiancée! Tri Ton was a good place to make such accusations.'

The young man heard no sounds after the two gun-shots. Blood soaked through his thick khaki jacket; he knew he was in extreme danger. Not able to protect his fiancee, he rolled as quickly as he could along the dam, sliding into the mud and water. Darkness must have protected him for many hours until he found himself stiff in the middle of the mud along the river bank.

The patient was transferred from the recovery room to a supposed prison cell. It was a small wooden shack within the hospital area for sick prisoners who were still in medical care, but were not allowed to stay in a normal ward. It was the most unusual thing I had ever seen. He was not allowed to see anybody. He was transferred to the Vietnamese nursing staff and those treating him medically had to be checked by the security guard regularly.

Susan, with her own money, bought a mosquito net, a thermos, a cup, a large tin of biscuits and some other small things. Together we made a visit without a permit to the patient in the hospital cell. The security guard was con-scious of his responsibility, but saw Susan as a nurse doing her duty. He opened the cell for us. It was actually like a box of matches, the size of a double bed with a rough wooden floor, not high enough even to sit straight up. The heat in the middle of the day was overwhelming.

The patient was sitting as if he was having a steam bath. Our earlier joy over the improvement of our patient sud-denly disappeared. I realised that the patient had started a new ordeal. The medical care now was almost complete;

this man would soon be sent to a real prison. It would be worse than this place.

'Here's something for you to use,' the nurse said, clearing her throat. 'I'll come back again to see how you are.' Her voice seemed to melt in the heat and dissolve in the air. The patient, like a bird in a cage, did not respond. His eyes were red and wet. I did not know whether he was sweating because of the heat, or was it his tears? Urged by the guard, we left immediately.

Two days later, Susan and I came back. The guard was not there. Over the barbed wire fence we saw a huge lock hanging outside the shack. We knew the patient had been taken away.

Shortly afterwards, a woman appeared at the hospital. People recognised that she was not from among the local people. She was very young — about nineteen — and very attractive. She wore a set of black *ba ba* (a peasant outfit), a pair of thongs on her dusty feet, and a *non la* (a hat made of lantana leaves) in her hand. She unobtrusively tried to ask for information about the man from Tri Ton. It surprised me that she did not intend to obtain the information from the hospital office; instead, she talked quietly to people around the ward.

I recalled the patient and his words about his fiancee, about my offer to help him if I saw someone looking for him. I hesitated to talk to her. I was concerned for my own security. Was this young lady simply the man's fiancee? Was she a kind of contact for Viet Cong in town? Who was the young man really? Was he a government soldier or the enemy? Why had the other man tried to kill him? Was it simply because he wanted to marry a beautiful woman? Or was the shooting part of the war?

I did not think this young woman was actually a Viet Cong just because she came from a Viet Cong stronghold area. She seemed to me too beautiful and vulnerable to be involved in such inhuman actions. Deep inside me I wanted to be helpful and tell her that I knew of her, that the young man had been taken to gaol, to warn her not to arouse suspicion in this town. However, I remained silent — I often wondered whether she was genuine.

On the way home from work that evening, I walked across the small bridge which linked the two areas at the heart of this provincial town. The bridge was short and narrow. I could see the friendly people who lived here travelling home from work. A Vietnamese doctor, a public servant from the government administrative office, some Vietnamese military people in a jeep with their American allies, the Australian team in their white Holden station wagon. Everybody waved at each other pleasantly as if we were part of the family. Life seemed kind and loving at a moment like this.

I could hardly believe that after a normal night's sleep, I would wake up to see more people lying restlessly in the hospital beds, dying. From many hidden places around my homeland, people continued to kill each other, whereas others from outside tried to save and heal, and still others tried to live a normal life. Then there were thousands of others like me who were confused and ignorant about the events around them.

Bearing in mind what I was told by the American major about the Australian accent, it always surprised me how I managed to understand the Australian doctors and nurses; it was more likely to be little cultural things that sometimes drove us crazy.

Ann Boucher was a theatre nurse and was also responsible for the team's residence management. We both had just come back to the team's house from the hospital. Everything was new and unfamiliar to both the Australians and the Vietnamese at this stage. Ann needed me to pass on some instructions to her household staff. I was exhausted from long hours of talking to the patients, and now, in the midday heat, I was longing for a glass of cold water to cool me down.

'Would you like a drink?' Ann asked, opening the refrigerator.

Suddenly my sensitive culture whispered to me, 'This is Ann's home and you are just a new friend to her; it's not courteous if you accept the drink right away. She should offer you something to drink without asking you!' I was always shy and I felt awkward; and my answer was a traditional courtesy. 'Hmm. . . I think I'm all right. . .!'

'Are you sure, Phuong?'

It was not a day of leisure and we were both in a hurry to go back to work. Ann finished her orange juice quickly and closed the fridge. 'O dear!' I silently cried. 'I do want a drink!'

When we were in the car driving back to the hospital, Ann said to me, 'Perhaps you're used to the heat. I felt terribly hot and I drink constantly!'

I did not say a word to her. When I passed the corridor of the hospital surgery suite I saw a little girl playing around the corner. 'Hullo, miss!' The girl had been in the hospital for a while to look after her sick mother, and became friendly with us all.

I stopped her and said, 'Please run and buy me an iced coffee, dear!' And I handed her some money. For a while I wondered why Ann — normally a thoughtful person — did not offer me a drink that day.

Pre-operation Ward 3 became very crowded with different kinds of sicknesses. Both Vietnamese and Australian staff were extremely busy; small things relating to the patients before and after surgery became everybody's job.

Ann was working mainly in the operating theatre. She knew very little about the Vietnamese patients in their everyday lives.

'Nam, a male patient is supposed to have a surgical examination under anaesthetic now. But I see no men in the ward. They're all women!'

I took the medical papers from Ann's hand and walked alongside the beds. A man rose up in anticipation on a bed around the corner. 'Miss! Miss! It's me here!' I stopped at his bed, looked at him and the patient's name on the papers. Suddenly I burst into laughter. I knew why Ann could not recognise this patient. The Vietnamese peasants, male and female, often wear the same traditional peasant outfit, a set of black or white fabric *ba ba*. Some men also wear their hair long and tied into a chignon at the back of their heads. It was certainly not easy to identify them when they were in bed and not talking.

This man could not understand why Ann passed by his bed several times and he tried to make signs that he was aware of his 'surgical check' today and was waiting for it; but she kept walking away from him. 'Because I thought he was a woman!' Ann whispered to me and giggled.

The war intensified and affected not only soldiers in the battlefields, but also innocent people. It caused suffering, sickness, hardship and poverty. The Australian team had now stretched their working time to late at night. They watched over the patients during weekends. At last the doctor and the interpreters decided to launch into a different kind of battle to fight to save human life. In addition to their normal duties, some members of the surgical team formed a medical team to help overcome the side effects of the war on people. An outpatient practice opened daily in the care of an Australian physician and an interpreter.

An influx of people with all sorts of problems came into

this section of the hospital every day. Most of these people were from different provinces, from remote villages and hamlets. They travelled a long way to this province and had to wait around for a week for their turn, hoping to see the Australian doctors and have caring treatment free. They had no place of refuge while waiting. They slept in every corner of the town and in the empty marketplace.

I had always enjoyed working with and helping people, but this was a special experience. In the heat of an endless summer, amidst the boisterous sounds of the crowds outside the outpatient ward, the doctor, after raising the first routine question with a patient — 'How long has he been sick?' — suddenly grumbled annoyingly, 'Phuong, what's all this about? I only asked him one simple question! Why do you take so long to find out? We have about a hundred people waiting outside!'

The upset of not being able to explain the problem in a short time stuck in my throat. I almost shouted at the woman who was sitting opposite me and in front of the doctor after she answered the above question with 'I'm sick long ago, miss!'

'Long ago is how long?' I said each word slowly to get her attention.

'Let's see. . . It was the last harvest time in my village!'

'Can you just tell me if it's four months, six months, or one year — something like that?'

The woman looked confused. She opened her left hand, used her thumb to touch the tip of the other fingers one by one and counted, 'One, two. . .'

I looked at the doctor in frustration. 'I do not have any idea when the last harvest time was in her village. But that's when she got sick!' Then I made a joke to the doctor. 'It's up to you, doctor! You decide how long she's been sick. If you want me to interpret immediately what the patient says, it means you have to guess a lot of things from them.'

I was hoping someone better would be the next patient so that I would not have the same problem again. The door opened and another figure squeezed in, an ailing man with a long beard and long hair tied back. The doctor looked at the patient, pulled down his lower eyelids and asked, 'How old is he?'

'I'm the Year of the Rat, miss!'

'Oh dear me!' At that moment I felt as if quitting the job was better than working out exactly how old he was for the doctor. I wished I had the most modern calculator to work out quickly the Chinese horoscope years, because 'the Rat' could be 1900, 1912 or 1924. Which year was suitable for him according to his tired look? And I grumbled to myself, 'Doctor, why do you need to ask him? Just use your magic stethoscope and you would know everything!'

A Vietnamese friend and colleague replaced me at out-patients in order to give me relief. But doing the ward rounds with the doctors and nurses did not help. More details were needed from the patients to make an accurate diagnosis and treatment for them.

'Is there a dispensary close to where you live?'

'Yes.'

'How close is it?'

'From my home? I guess it's about. . . finishing a cigarette, miss!'

I didn't know how to express my frustration! I turned to the Ward Chief Nurse for help. She burst into laughter. 'Only Buddha knows what they meant! These terms are used a lot by countryside people to express their way of life. I guess the answer.'

Next to this man was another patient on his bed

anxiously waiting for his turn. He tried to help me by correcting this man. 'It's not that far, friend! It's only about throwing a stone!' Then he turned to me. 'Believe me, miss! I lived near him!' I almost choked. I thought, 'It's not the Australian accent that is difficult; but it's my lack of understanding of my own people.' The doctors and nurses were all exasperated with this kind of conversation with the Vietnamese country-side patients.

The next day as I was resting at the surgeon's office in the surgical suite after a hectic morning around the wards, my friend suddenly appeared. He shook his head constantly. 'Phuong, do you have a headache tablet?' He dropped himself down in a chair and said, 'What kind of Vietnamese did you teach the Australian doctor in the outpatients?'

'What's happened? What did I do wrong?' I stared at him in surprise.

But as soon as I had asked the friend, I burst into laughter. I realised what might have happened to upset him. To save time and to meet the needs of the large number of patients waiting outside every day, the doctor had asked me to teach him some basic phrases in Vietnamese so that he could talk directly to the patients when he examined them. Phrases like *tho manh* (take a deep breath), *nin tho* (hold your breath), *nam xuong* (lie down), *ngoi day* (sit up). And so the doctor practised and used them. He had meant to ask the woman to take a deep breath for him and exhale, but he kept saying '*Nin tho, Nin tho,*' 'Hold your breath.'

'I said *nin tho*!' the doctor said, raising his voice impatiently.

But finally when the woman could no longer hold her breath as she was told by the doctor in Vietnamese, she exhaled, her face red.

'Why didn't you do that in the beginning?' the doctor moaned.

I guessed the doctor, my friend and the patient all had had a hard time!

*   *   *

The shadows of evening fell slowly on the trees, on the street and down to the water under the bridge. A light breeze filled the air bringing from somewhere the gentle fragrance of jasmine and magnolias. I always enjoyed the relaxing atmosphere of the evening in this town, away from the busy demanding life inside the hospital. But it was already late to be walking home this evening. I felt reluctant to take myself home after leaving Dr Thinh's office only a few minutes earlier.

Dr Thinh was a man in his mid-forties, chief of the provincial Ministry of Health and also the head of the provincial hospital. Dr Thinh, though he was the highest authority at the hospital, was a soft, gently-spoken man who had both the respect and love of the people he met.

I was asked to see him at his office that afternoon after work. Dr Thinh told me, 'Miss Phuong, your work with the team to help the hospital has been highly regarded by us all. I have no reason to stop you from your commitment to the poor. However I would like to ask you to slow down your work at the outpatients to only a minimum level.'

I was deeply hurt. Deep inside I always felt very proud of being helpful to my people; and here I was asked not to work hard for them. 'Why is that, doctor, may I ask?' I pleaded, confused.

Dr Thinh understood my concern. Smiling at me pleasantly, he invited me to try the hot Chinese tea he had placed in front of me on his desk. 'The influx every day of outpatients to this hospital has driven the province to distraction with its security management. In fact this seems to be developing to a level which is actually going against the anti-VC policy of the government.'

'But how? I certainly don't understand, doctor.'

Dr Thinh continued. 'Especially the increase in patients with chest complaints who ask for antibiotics!'

'But doctor, the Australian team explained to me that in this war situation the Vietnamese have not been provided with any kind of health care. It's important to give them a check and of course the doctors give antibiotics only to people who have got TB.'

Still with a pleasant manner, Dr Thinh sat up straight in his chair and lowered his voice. 'Can I trust you and tell you this secret? I was told that the outpatient section has been watched by the secret police for suspected Viet Cong. Rumour has spread around that the Vietcong in their stronghold areas have been forcing innocent people to see *Bac si Uc Dai Loi* (Australian doctors) with chest complaints to get as many antibiotics as they can to sell to them at cheap prices. Others are forced to give to them freely. I know that only the real TB patients receive antibiotics for treatment; but even so they are not permitted to keep the medicines for themselves. The Viet Cong need these medicines while they are living in the jungle.'

This revelation created a conflict for me. I felt angry at the people who had undermined this expression of good-will and who made their own people suffer. I left the office without saying goodbye to Dr Thinh in the correct manner. I walked home in deep anguish. I thought I must quit this job.

The next morning I went to the outpatient ward again. I said to the Australian doctor I was not feeling very well. 'Then I won't make you work too hard today, Phuong,' the doctor kindly said to me. I wished at that moment I could be as trustful as the Australian doctor.

When I passed the X-ray room, a peasant woman suddenly rushed out from a corner and greeted me warmly. I looked at her and remembered that she was the mother of a three-year-old boy who had died of meningitis at the hospital some time before. When the child was first brought in for an X-ray, I used the Vietnamese common term *chup hinh* (literally, 'taking picture') to explain to the mother what the doctor was going to do for her child. Unfortunately, despite the great effort from the team, the child had died tragically afterwards.

'Hello, miss! Do you recognise me, miss?' The woman smiled happily.

'Of course I remember you!' I clapped her gently on the shoulder and said, 'How are you? What brings you here today?'

'I came to ask you for a favour, miss. I'd like to have the picture the doctor took of my little boy. I hope you don't mind helping me! I miss my son so much, but I don't have anything as a memory of him. Life has been so hard that we haven't had any chance to do good things for him; even having a picture taken of him before he got sick.'

My eyes welled with tears. I explained to her it was not the sort of photograph which was normally taken for people to keep as a memory. It was only taken inside a child's head for the doctors to see what caused the sickness; and the real face of the child did not show on the film. But the woman was not able to understand me; she wandered around the hospital the whole day hoping I would have time to do this special favour for her.

How sad I was for this underprivileged woman, a picture of countless Vietnamese people who have suffered in endless hardship and poverty caused by war and ambition. People might think she was a fool, but deep in her heart she was a beautiful mother. I said to this loving woman I would ask the Australian doctors and nurses to pose with her in front of the surgery suite for a photograph for her as a memento of her son. This did not satisfy her.

Again I came to outpatients. In the hot sun among the crowd a voice burst out, 'It's her turn today. I'm glad it's her. Without her careful explanation I wouldn't remember how to use the medicines as soon as I get home.'

Then I said to myself, 'I'll stay though it's hard.'

7

East-West romance: 1965 – 1969

I WAS WALKING WITH PETER RYAN, the surgeon and leader of the new surgical team, to the hospital pharmacy. Over the hos-pital front gate on the street, a cheer went up from a group of school children. *'My! My!'* 'American! American!' *'Hullo, Ong My!'*, 'Mr American!'

The children laughed happily, pointing at Peter. This was a friendly thing and happened almost everywhere in Vietnam during the war, especially in the countryside. Children assumed any European person seen in this country was American. Peter suddenly stopped me from walking further and came close to the children. 'Please explain to them we're not American. We're Australian doctors.'

'Not *My*?' A boy looked at Mr Ryan from head to toe, surprised. 'Same, same! I don't understand!'

Peter smiled warmly, seized a bit of his dark brown wavy hair parted a little too far to one side and said, 'Look at this, boys! Long hair and white clothes! Not crewcut hair and green clothes! Got it?'

'Okay! Okay! Not crewcut hair!' The boy repeated cheer-fully after Peter. But the same boy, probably thirteen and the oldest, suddenly asked, 'Doctor, chewing gum? Chew-

ing gum?' His eyes peered into the doctor's shirt pocket.
'No? No chewing gum! No good! No good! Let's go, kids!'

And they all ran away from us.

Dressed in white short-sleeve shirt and shorts and white
shoes and socks, the men of the new team in their uniforms
looked much like a first grade sports team rather than a
medical team. They were from St Vincent's Hospital in
Melbourne.

The Royal Melbourne team by this time had finished
their one-year stint — from October 1964 to November 1965
— in this provincial hospital. The memories of working
with the first team were still fresh with me.

Mr Macleish, the team leader, used to use his short
break between two operations for a short visit to a sick
patient about whom he was concerned. One day he said
gently to a little boy who looked lonely, 'Come here, little
man!' The boy looked shy but moved forward to him.
'Can you do this?' He sat down on his feet.

The boy stared at him. Mr Macleish's face looked
serious and his left hand held his lower jaw. 'Are you
ready?' he asked. All of a sudden as he slapped his right
hand gently but quickly on his head, his tongue stuck out
of his mouth between his teeth. It was as if the tongue was
chopped off by the teeth! He played it so well that nobody
could see the cleverness of the fun game. The little boy
burst into laughter. The boy practised again and again until
I saw him do it in front of his sick father beside his bed.

The surgeon's willingness to make a child laugh and a
patient smile was a comfort in this war-ravaged country.

The friendliness of the Australian team brought them
and the local Vietnamese together on many happy occasions. Macleish had performed a massive gastrectomy
on a Mr Huu. In appreciation, his family organised a
dinner where the Australian team were served with many

authentic traditional dishes including roasted young pigeons. Suddenly Mr Macleish gently put his chopsticks on the table and said, 'I surrender!' He whispered, 'Is it possible for me to use my own chopsticks, Phuong?' I stared at him surprised. He clapped his thumb and first finger together and smiled at me. I burst into laughter, 'Of course you can, doctor!' We ate, laughed and enjoyed our time as if we were one people without cultural barriers.

At another time the team was invited by my parents to our place where they all enjoyed my mother's special dishes — charcoal-grilled trout with home-made mayonnaise and chicken stewed with Oriental herbs.

This team could be trusted. But as the influx of foreign allies to the country increased, the large cities such as Saigon, Danang and Cam Ranh became centres of moral conflict.

A girlfriend of mine got a job working at one of the MACV (US Military Assistance Command Vietnam) offices in Saigon. She finally admitted to me, 'You're lucky working among trusted people.' Substantial American wealth had provided opportunities for Vietnam to become better in some aspects; but it had also fostered in the society many corrupt practices, materially and morally.

Young women were greatly concerned at being mistaken by others about their relations to foreigners. I had to make sure my relationship with the Australian team was not interpreted wrongly by the local community. I tried whenever I could to let people know my work was with 'the Australian doctors', so it helped when a badge was introduced with a tiny skipping kangaroo gilded in the corner on a green base.

Towards the end of 1965 and early 1966 I began to work with the new Australian team. One of my duties was to assist the physician in the outpatient unit which was a room as small as a box of matches, with an entrance and a window covered with an old fabric curtain. Inside was a small desk for the doctor, a single bed for the patients' examination and several wooden chairs. It was a simple facility provided by the hospital for the team to see the patients. The new doctor — a Dr Jones — requested the room be cleaned up with everything changed. Even a flower vase was brought in and put on the working table.

One Monday morning, as usual, I was arranging for the first patient to come in for examination. Dr Jones said, 'Don't be in too much of a hurry. It's only Monday. We have plenty of time!'

'Sorry. What are you saying, doctor?' I was surprised. Working in this place always meant hurrying; no previous doctor seemed as relaxed as this doctor was.

'Did you have a good weekend?' he asked.

'Yes, I did. And you, doctor?' I answered him.

He seemed a little hesitant. 'Do you often go to Saigon for shopping?'

'Only occasionally,' I answered, but felt this man a little strange. 'Everything is ready, doctor. Should I start with the first patient?' I was anxious for the hundreds of patients who were waiting outside.

'I see that you don't have a watch. Would you like me to buy one for you?' I had never heard this kind of offer from any Australian doctors or nurses, even from Susan, my best girlfriend on the team.

'Thankyou, doctor. I have a watch.'

'But I don't see you wearing it. Is it broken? I'll buy you a new one anyway.' He paused for a little while and said, 'It's no problem for me at all! There are plenty of things that I can buy for you in Saigon.'

'Thankyou. That's very kind of you. But I've never thought of it.' I became suspicious of the doctor's behaviour.

'Let's work!' He urged me to call the first patient. 'And you think about it and let me know.'

The whole day I observed the doctor's attitude. But I could not understand him. A few days later he asked me if I would like to go to Saigon for shopping that weekend. He could arrange the flight for me. I became worried, but refused him nicely by saying that when I needed to I would ask him, but at present I didn't need anything from him.

After a week's work that I found unaccountably difficult, he came into the outpatients' room one morning wearing fresh white clothes and a little perfume. In his hand he had something like a gift box. He sat down on the edge of the bed when I was sitting at the desk viewing the patients' registration cards. His voice sounded very nervous. 'Would you like to be sinful with me on the bed, miss?'

I stared at him. I did not know if I understood him correctly. Perspiration soaked my dress. 'Come on! Don't be shy! It's wonderful!' he urged as he unbuttoned his shirt.

I felt faint. I rushed out of the room and ran towards the surgery unit where most of the team was working. From behind I still heard from the crowd, 'What's happening? She's not well today? Is she coming back?'

The doctor dismissed the crowd and went to work quietly around the ward. I told the team leader that I was not well and went home without telling anybody the truth.

For the following week, Dr Jones gave me an unbelievably hard time. He blamed me for every little thing which was considered normal by other doctors. He even said that I was not qualified to work with him. I asked Peter Ryan if I could change my work to the surgery, but I was too embarrassed to tell him the reason. He sensed that something had gone wrong at the outpatient unit. He wanted to know the reason before he could help me. Tears welled up and words stuck in my throat each time I was about to speak the truth.

Peter Ryan asked Nancy, the ward sister and probably the oldest among the nurses in the team, to find out the truth from me. I broke my silence and Nancy was shocked. A few weeks later Dr Jones disappeared from the hospital. I was told he had been sent back to Australia.

It was a hurtful experience, but I was thankful for the understanding and delicacy of the leader to restore my confidence in working with the team. Jeanette, a Vietnamese working for the team as a cook, used to be married to a Frenchman and was a straightforward outspoken person.

'How do you know these men are good clean people?' some asked her.

'How do I know?' A sharp voice was heard from Jeanette. 'I've worked for foreigners — French and American — for many years. Frankly, I could not avoid knowing the bad side of them. But I've seen nothing, not a sign of that sort of thing from these men. They're working really hard. They really represent the good.'

Several weeks later, a new young physician arrived, Dr Bruce Kelly. I began working in the outpatient unit again with the new doctor. Despite the high demand of work in the surgery unit, Peter Ryan often came to the crowded outpatient unit 'to see if you both are still surviving under the heat', on one occasion drawing out from both pockets two bottles of Coca Cola. We all laughed happily. I felt the world was one again.

Bruce Kelly was in his late twenties. He was rather tall — about 170 centimetres — with fair hair and brown eyes. He looked no different to the other Australians I had met. After working with him for a while I became convinced of his sincerity and dedication. He was the kind of person who could look straight into your eyes and say, 'I am a good man — trust me.' And you would believe him. The trouble with the other doctor made me careful in my meetings with him. But his gentleness towards me deeply impressed me.

What did this really mean? Was it the beginning of a romance? I was confused. I thought of my father, his religious belief, and my explicit intention to be a good child of my parents.

No, I had tried to avoid any complexity in my life which might cause disappointment to him. For a while I truly hoped the feeling I had for the new doctor was only misunderstanding. However, the sudden presence of the doctor on my night duty at the hospital was a source of happiness for myself, a relief for the duty nurse in the intensive-care ward and a joy for all the patients of an evening.

'Phuong, please call me Bruce,' the doctor smiled and insisted. 'Can I be your friend and visit you at the hospital on your night duty?' I sensed in Bruce's words something which was warmer than friendship. It was like an intriguing touch to the softest spot of my heart, and it was hard to refuse. And so Bruce made regular visits to me each time I was on duty at the hospital.

Unless bombs were heard exploding not too far from our town, or rocket shells were seen lighting up the sky, I had almost forgotten that the violent war was actually around me.

Often in the evenings we stood against the brick railing built along the porch of the post-operation ward, looking over the green grass to the centre of the hospital yard, talking until the evening was worn out. We shared with each other about the contrasts of war and peace, about his family and mine, and about our faith in God. There was nothing romantic about the scene — not a candlelight or a red rose to add to our surroundings, not a sound of music to back up the conversation, not a drop of wine to sweeten our words. But the attractiveness was the mutual esteem that enfolded us and the symmetry of two young people from East and West.

Almost every hour of the evening, Bruce and I made our way among the patients' beds tangled with worn-out mosquito nets, blankets and mattresses to check on the condition of very sick patients. Bruce became available for most urgent cases at night in the hospital when he was with me. This 'off-time' job of Bruce's was certainly a great help to the hospital night staff.

While my emotions were lifted up by Bruce's special friendship, I never contemplated telling my parents about us. I always found it hard to make a decision. The attempt to step out of my present situation sounded to me as hard as moving a mountain; but being a romantic I often dreamed that I would be able to change the whole world according to my liking.

Bruce one day asked me, 'What does a man do when he wants to marry a woman according to your tradition?'

'Why do you need to know about it?' I replied with a smile on my heart.

'I love you, Phuong. I want to marry you. I think you love me, too. We must work things out for our marriage soon.'

Strangely, my reaction was, instead of excitement and joy, a slight withdrawal. 'It's a very sensitive and complicated matter. It needs the delicacy of a person who is well-known and highly respected by both families to act as the go-between. This is very important at the beginning; and there are more traditions to follow later. Bruce, I don't think you can arrange these things easily.'

My answer was like placing a barrier before him. This

is how I was and still am! My heart always urges me to be my own self, to be adventurous, to enjoy the benefits life offers; yet my mind encourages me to be comfortable where I am if that would make my parents happy!

My first serious courting came when I was seventeen, with someone from the same religious background as mine, but from central Vietnam. Other suitors came from strong Buddhist backgrounds; and my Christian background became the dark shadow on their future plans. Though these people knew the family I was from, they hoped that being a woman I would be able to walk away from my tradition for the sake of my marriage.

In an Asian family the sons, especially the eldest, must never break the Buddhist or Confucian tradition to marry a woman of a Western religion and be influenced by her. Men are to carry on the family's lineage and to be accountable for venerating their ancestors. But there is a traditional exception for a woman if there is no other choice.

My family, however, did not follow this cultural tradition, but did what we thought right according to our faith. Moreover I always hoped I would be able to convert the man who loved me to become a Christian. I later realised how naive I was about this binding Asian tradition which is deep-rooted in the blood and minds of most people of the East.

I received a note from Mrs Nhi who invited me to a meal at her home one evening. The note explained it would be a simple friendly evening with just herself and her husband, and there was nothing to worry about. Mrs Nhi was the wife of Dr Nhi, the gynaecologist and obstetrician at the provincial hospital. She herself was a lawyer who had a permanent practice in Saigon. Both Dr Nhi and his wife were in their mid-thirties, educated in France, sophisticated and highly respected in town.

Though I had been friendly with Dr Nhi while working at the hospital I had not had a chance to meet his wife. Her invitation was a surprise. I could not think of any reason better than there must be another warning about my work with the team, like Dr Thinh's to me a few months before.

During the evening, however, I was told that Bruce had finally shared with them his love for me. He asked Dr Nhi and his wife to be the go-between for him as Vietnamese tradition required. They planned to visit my parents for this purpose. Though overwhelmed, I was tortured by questions: Am I really getting married to a foreigner? Does it sound normal to everybody? How do my parents feel? What is the attitude of the church towards me and my parents?

'I'm afraid my father will not agree to my marrying a Westerner. He would consider this a big embarrassment! The church would think I'm not a good girl, if you understand what I really mean,' I told Mrs Nhi. 'In fact, I think it would be best if my father does not know of this matter at all.'

'Phuong! Please listen to me! There's nothing wrong about this whatsoever. He's an educated person with a brilliant career and he loves you! I'm sure your parents will be delighted.'

In confidence, Mrs Nhi pursued her purpose of the evening. 'Phuong, all I want from you tonight is to know for sure if you also love Bruce and would like to marry him. It's important. Leave all the rest to me!'

Until then I had had no chance to observe Mrs Nhi. She was very attractive, brilliant and energetic. There was no doubt she was also an effective lawyer. I felt as if I had just been fitted with those 'fairy slippers'. It was alluring and exquisite. It was something outside of me and untouchable; yet it appeared everywhere, in front of my eyes and on everything.

To Mrs Nhi my marriage to the doctor was only a simple matter of her special visit to my parents. 'You're twenty-seven, aren't you, Phuong? And he's also twenty-seven! And both are Christians! Perfect!' Mrs Nhi stated while adding some more crystal ice cubes to my drink.

I felt it better if I discussed with my mother and sisters what had happened to me and Bruce before Mrs Nhi met my father. It is always a great comfort to have a family that is willing to hear the most intimate things of our heart. Khue, my other married sister, lived too far away. All others were still too young. But Tuyet and Tram were thrilled for my future. However, above the excitement I could see a little cloud in everybody's eyes. We all sensed the difficulty, though nobody tried to speak about it. Hope and worries crossed each other in our minds.

'It's important not to let anybody know about this at the moment; especially the people from the church. I must talk to your father before Mrs Nhi does. This is not all that easy!' my mother said.

'We'll try to explain to Papa. Everything's going to be great!' Tuyet sounded hopeful. She was the eldest daughter, and was trusted by our parents.

'He's a doctor. Nobody is better! I think you should press Papa a little in this case, Mama!' Tram was excited and anxious.

'But it's not easy for your father to accept the idea of giving a daughter away to a white man!' my mother admitted. 'You know very well about "the American trend" as it's called these days. Common people could think all sorts of bad things are involved in this matter. Phuong trusts him and Mrs Nhi trusts him; but how does your father explain to the church that this is a good marriage? In fact, we know nothing much about this doctor.'

'But Mama, he's not American! He's Australian!' Tram, my younger sister, reminded my mother. 'We can trust him because of the good reputation of the Australian team in this town. They're educated people.'

Our conversation in the kitchen stopped suddenly when my father came in.

The special visit of Mrs Nhi to my father was to take place at 4.00 p.m. Tuyet travelled from her province to be with me on this special occasion. I took the afternoon off from the hospital. Bruce was working, but was anxious to hear from me and Mrs Nhi. My mother had prepared a delightful afternoon tea in the living room. A joyful and hopeful excitement filled the air in my home.

Mrs Nhi was greeted warmly by my parents. The introduction was formal and courteous, followed by selected fresh fruit, hot jasmine tea and home-made biscuits. The main talk then began.

From our bedroom I suddenly heard my father's voice, serious and determined. 'The doctor needs to become a Christian by attending our church regularly for at least six months; then he has to be baptised by our church before the wedding can be approved!'

'Excuse me, Pastor. I don't think Bruce needs to go through all those things again. Bruce is a Christian and was baptised by his Catholic church!'

'I'm so sorry about this, Mrs Nhi. But I would prefer him to do these things according to my church's tradition!'

'Why, Pastor? Why waste our time?' Mrs Nhi seemed a little nervous.

'No, it's important, Mrs Nhi! Because I must admit I'm still in doubt about whether or not a Catholic would receive salvation!' My father sounded serious.

Mrs Nhi was shocked. She was a Catholic. Her voice trembled. 'I'm sorry, Pastor. Do you really mean we

Catholics are not Christians? I'm afraid you don't have the right to judge who's wrong and who's right!'

I was unaware that this was an issue for my father. My mother originally was from the Catholic Church. Her father was not satisfied with some aspects of Catholic teaching and practice, so he joined the Reformed Church. But it was before I was born and I had never thought it could become a problem for me.

'I'm sorry I have to say this, but if you come to the high priest to receive repentance and believe he will forgive you on behalf of God, or if you pray to the saints and to the statues in your church including Mary's, I'm afraid you're wrong! Jesus Christ is the only bridge. . .'

'Sorry, Pastor!' Mrs Nhi interrupted nervously. 'Please reconsider our conversation this afternoon. I'm afraid we're on the wrong subject. I'm not here for a religious session!'

'Yes, I appreciate your purpose in being here this afternoon. But what I have said is very important, especially for the man who's going to marry my daughter.'

From my room I heard the movement of chairs and shoes and Mrs Nhi pressed her words gently but firmly. 'I guess you have your own business and I have mine. I've made a mistake in interfering in your family affairs. I'm really sorry. I'll tell the doctor everything. Goodbye, Pastor.'

She left immediately without saying a word to me or to the rest of my family. The supposed happy marriage proposal had become an argument over religion. When thinking back to those moments of my life, I thought my father had not acted as a father, but as a religious extremist; and Mrs Nhi was not a sensitive go-between, but a pragmatic lawyer! For my father, the desire of winning a soul was as strong as winning a court case for Mrs Nhi. Neither of them wanted to lose!

Dinner at my home was normally the happiest time of

the day. But that evening was tense. Hundreds of thoughts went through my mind after Mrs Nhi left our home. What would I say to Bruce tomorrow? Would he be angry at my father? Would he still love me and try to do what my father wanted?

My father was still working at his desk in the front room at midnight that night. This had been a common scene in our home for as long as I can remember. My father committed his day to visiting, counselling and helping the people of his church. This was as important as preaching. He used the most quiet hours of the night to work on his sermons, to seek God's teaching for him and for his church. When the family woke up around six in the morning, my father was already at his desk.

That night in bed, while my mind was in turmoil, I overheard my parents arguing in the front room.

'You know how right it is for a young woman to get married and settle down with a family of her own. I'm concerned that your unbending attitude has let this opportunity pass for Phuong.'

The silence filled the air for a while, then came my father's voice. 'But what can I do other than ask him to do what the church requires? I can't be easier because it's my daughter. Moreover, if I don't make everything very clear, this marriage may cause misunderstanding about the Asian woman's virtue in this area. I find it so strange to have a foreigner as a son-in-law! You know how different East is from West!'

'But if that's how Phuong's life turns out, we have to be happy for her and support her. I feel we've missed this kind of opportunity for our girls ever since we volunteered to take up responsibility for this small town church instead of that large congregation in Saigon.'

My father had been asked to go to a large congregation,

but the urgent needs of this provincial church touched my father's heart. From then on, ever since people gossipped about my parents not being sensitive to the needs of their growing girls, I sensed my father was upset. I heard him push his chair back and address my mother in a high-pitched voice: 'What do you mean "we have to be happy for her and support her"? Does it mean to let her go to the doctor? Or would her wedding take place in the Catholic church? It's impossible!'

'No, no, I don't mean that. To me there's nothing wrong about him being a foreigner. The Catholic matter I think we could work out later!'

'Is that what you've been planning with her?'

I wished to get out of bed and say to my father, 'I love you, Papa! But we can't be and don't wish to be an example for anybody. We've got our own lives to live.' However I kept silent. To an Asian family, being a good child meant letting one's parents work out everything for one's life.

My father suddenly lowered his voice. 'You seem to have taken total responsibility for this matter. She's also your daughter. You feel free to do what you want for her. I'll stand aside! And remember! I will have to resign as a church minister if things from my own family do not happen the way they should.'

*   *   *

I paid the cyclo driver and walked to the entrance of the Australian house. It was just before six in the morning. All around me was still quiet. Looking for Bruce at this hour was the most daring thing I had ever done. But I just had to see Bruce immediately and tell him what had happened at my home yesterday, especially the shocking argument between my parents the previous night. At last I found strength and walked inside. I knocked at his door.

'Yes! Who is it?'

'It's me, Bruce! It's Phuong!'

The door opened and I slipped into the room. Bruce was already up and dressed. Like me, he could not sleep all night after Mrs Nhi rang him. The disappointment from my news was clear on his face. His restless manner showed in every movement. He had struggled over the same bitter feelings.

'Your father is ridiculous! Why does he follow such a tradition? I don't have much time left in Vietnam. . . Doesn't he realise that?' He paused for a moment, 'But if I do have time I certainly won't agree to such a. . .!'

'Such a what?' For the first time my pride in my own parents, especially my father, filled my head. I said to Bruce bitterly, 'It doesn't matter whether he's ridiculous or not. If you feel you can't do what my father wishes, I'm afraid I can't get married to you. I can't afford to see my father resign from the church!'

The lamp from the table shed a soft light around the small room. The cosy sleepy feeling was still there. We were so close at this moment; yet the deep prejudices between East and West might tear us apart tomorrow! Though I sounded firm in those last words, my mind dreamt of Bruce and me escaping from these plights, living free and enjoying our life together.

'I'm so sorry, Phuong,' I suddenly heard Bruce whisper. 'I should not have said such things about your father. I love you. I must try again.'

A glow of hope filled my mind when Bruce asked, 'Is there an American missionary working around this area?'

'Yes, I think so,' I answered him.

'I'm going there. I'll ask the missionary for help. Perhaps being a missionary and a Westerner who has been dealing with this culture he would know how to help us.'

That weekend Bruce drove 100 kilometres to meet the American missionary. Unfortunately the missionary's opinion was the same as my father's. Bruce's bitterness at religious prejudice was difficult to control.

Until then Bruce had never said he would give up the idea of marrying me. There was no other way, unless a simple wedding ceremony was arranged by ourselves at the registrar's office. But Bruce had never tempted me to do this nor had I ever wished to do such a thing against my parents. My mother was very concerned for me; but she knew it would be wrong if she tried to work it out alone. For three weeks my father and I did not talk to each other.

Shortly afterwards, Bruce left Vietnam to go back to Australia. My days without him became empty. *'Un seul être vous manque et tout est dépeuplé!'*, 'When someone who is dear to your heart is missing, the whole world turns to a desert!' Somewhere from the back of my mind this old French saying proved to be true. Gentle rains became like bitter tears and sunrays were only torture to my broken heart.

However, letters full of love and care from Bruce began flowing to me; each was like a kind of suture which gradually mended the hidden wound in my heart. Each night I slept on his letters of love and hope. They were like a soft pillow on which I survived through my winter.

One day Bruce wrote admitting to me that he had been facing a second plight, his mother's objection to his marriage to a Protestant and also an Asian. When Bruce had told her of his decision to join the Australian medical team to go to Vietnam, the country tortured by war, her tears were as bitter as the tears of a Vietnamese mother who had lost her son in battle. And when Bruce told her of his plan to go back there to marry a Vietnamese woman and a Protestant, the whole bright future she had hoped for him all of a sudden collapsed.

A close Australian girlfriend, a nurse from the team, wrote to me regularly. She told me about the crisis, a 'cold war' between Bruce and his mother over our problem. It was like having a kind of reversed culture shock for me. I had always believed that the East was more protective and conservative and that the freedom of the West had created independent minds which would accept diversity. I never predicted opposition from Bruce's family.

At last, broken-hearted, I wrote a final letter to Bruce to free us from each other for the sake of both our parents. I continued to work with many other Australian doctors and nurses who took turns to come to this province to fulfil the two countries' diplomatic responsibilities. However, nothing could fill the emptiness of my days without Bruce!

*   *   *

In the 1968 Lunar New Year known as the 'Tet Offensive', a thirty-six-hour ceasefire was agreed to by both the Vietnamese communist forces and the south Vietnamese government for the traditional New Year's celebration. This special agreement was deliberately exploited by the communists in order to seize the south. They broke their agreement and made major assaults on Saigon, Hue, Danang and indeed every province in the south. Rockets and mortars showered like thunderstorms upon anything, anywhere.

Within a few days, the New Year's 'ceasefire' had caused massive death and destruction, and left thousands of wounded people and countless homeless families. For a few days all provincial cities were on curfew. People were on alert for being evacuated to somewhere safer.

When the 'ceasefire' was finally over, it was apparent that our provincial town had escaped the fate planned by the communists and remained unharmed. The provincial police forces worked their best, and to the amazement of the whole local population they actually caught a Viet Cong liaison agent — a little boy of about twelve years old — who had with him a chart detailing the surprise attack planned for that night. The little boy somehow had lost his contact at the bus station. He had wandered around with a frightened look until he was caught.

The hospital during this time was overflowing with wounded soldiers and civilians from nearby provinces. In those days death walked side by side with the living. On one of my duty nights, at about 2.00 a.m., a trolley was suddenly wheeled into the theatre bringing a man wounded from a bomb explosion. I stood next to the patient waiting for the Australian doctor. 'Please help, doctor! Please help!' an old woman cried. My heart went out in a moment to this old mother. I pulled up the old blanket which covered the patient to see how he was. I touched his feet and my hand suddenly felt icy cold. He had died on the way from his remote village to the hospital, but his mother did not know.

Shortly after, I received a letter from Bruce in which he said, 'I have been praying for you, but feared that you might have been lost somewhere in the battle. Please write and tell me that you are safe!' His care for me brought tears to my heart.

I thought that there was something ridiculous being born in this troubled land. Yet it was my motherland where my heart belonged. It was just like Bruce's mother had wanted him to belong to his homeland. I could not deny my country nor should I expect to be taken away from her, even though it would be away from suffering.

Later I left the hospital and returned to my local USAID office for a short time. At the end of 1968 I moved to Saigon to join the field office of an international aid organisation.

Bruce went to Singapore. From there he wrote to me. Believing we were both old enough to make our own decision, he planned that if I would get a tourist visa to Singapore to meet him, we would get married. He was staying with a Chinese friend who had graduated in medicine in Australia. The Chinese doctor had married his Australian girlfriend and had a lovely little daughter. Bruce wrote, 'I am jealous of the happiness of my friend and regret that I have not yet overcome our own problem!' The anguish of leaving behind all my loved ones to go to another country tortured me for many days, but I was frozen by the idea that the church might not understand my eloping to get married.

My own romantic problems were set in the chaotic aftermath of the Tet Offensive. In Saigon, people's everyday lives were filled with fear and uncertainty. The communists practised many different forms of terrorism in order to undermine freedom and confuse the administration of the south in order to prepare for their invasion. 'Don't walk on the thick grass, don't play with used cans or bottles on the ground, don't hit a bundle along the road, don't sit in public places such as restaurants or cinemas.' These were the warnings the city people kept reminding each other and their children of.

Xe lam was a three-wheeled Lambretta vehicle commonly used for public transport in Saigon by ordinary people. There were no timetables, no schedules, no capacity limit, but low fares. In peak hours, it was a real challenge to fight for a seat, to get to where you wanted to on time. In this type of fight, very often I was the miserable loser among the long legs and hard muscles.

Early one morning, as usual, I was struggling among the passengers to get on one to go to work. My one foot was stuck with a lot of others on the vehicle's step. My other foot was still somewhere on the ground. Suddenly I felt myself pulled roughly off the vehicle. Immediately I released myself and stepped back on the street. It was nasty and disappointing, but not unusual. I stood back to wait for the next one. A few minutes later, all the people at the station and I were terrified to hear that the vehicle I had been getting on was blown up along Nguyen Du Street where I used to get off and walk to my office. It was destroyed by an explosive trapped somewhere underneath. There was one dead and many were injured.

One day Tuyet, my sister, and her husband made a trip from Dalat to Saigon. The trip took about six hours by bus on the national road through endless highland forest. They departed at midday and, after everything was settled down in the bus for the long journey, most of the passengers, including my sister and her husband, went to sleep. On the quiet winding road, a group of armed soldiers appeared and waved the bus to stop.

'All the ARVN (South Vietnamese Army) men get out for an ID check, please!' the leading soldier ordered. Most of the men got off the bus; but Tran, my sister's husband, was still soundly asleep. Tuyet woke him up by gently touching his arm. 'Wake up, wake up, darling!' Tran stayed asleep. All of a sudden, the leading soldier turned his gun on the driver and said, 'Get back on the bus and go! Quickly!' and he and his group shoved the men towards the jungle. At that moment the driver and passengers realised who these people were — Viet Cong terrorists posing as ARVN soldiers to ARVN men. Only Tran escaped the terrorism.

Despite these difficulties, life kept going. The south was still the centre of freedom. Saigon was still the living heart of its people and the focal point of those allied supporters who sought to alleviate suffering.

In mid 1969, Bruce came back to Vietnam for the second time and worked at Bien Hoa provincial hospital. Jenny Dyason — now Jenny Hunter, a theatre nurse who worked at the provincial hospital previously — came back to Bien Hoa for a second assignment. I met Bruce again with Jenny. Jenny wanted to help us to be together, and promised to care for me if I married Bruce and went to Australia. The old pressures which still weighed heavily on us, even though I was older and had been living away from my parents for some time now, made it too hard to say yes.

* * *

Some of my Australian friends wondered why most modern Vietnamese music sounds sad and sorrowful. Most of it was composed when the war was at its fiercest. This love song expresses the concern of a soldier husband who was leaving his young wife to go into battle:

Sweetheart! You asked me
If I would come back to you soon.
Yes, I will, very soon.
But I'll be lying on a stretcher,
Carried by a helicopter.
And when you hear it landing,
You'll greet me in a white scarf,
Twirled around your youthful hair.

Thu Lan was a petite young woman and head nurse of the pre-surgical ward in our provincial hospital. She was in her mid-twenties when she married Trong, a captain in the army, and they had a daughter. Not long after, Thu Lan was offered a one-year scholarship to go to the US for further nursing training. It was a real challenge, not only for Thu Lan and her husband, but also for the whole immediate family. With complete support from her husband and both sets of parents, Thu Lan left for the US.

Three months later, Trong was killed in a military mission far away from his home. He accidentally stepped on a VC booby-trap while leading ARVN troops in an operation searching for Vietcong. Thu Lan changed from being happy and chatty into a heartbroken young widow.

I went to her home the evening she arrived back from the US for her husband's funeral. Sitting dazed in an armchair in the corner of the living room near the coffin, Thu Lan looked just like the withered flowers on the national honour wreath which had accompanied the fallen soldier on his last journey home. The silence coming from the dead soldier was so immense that the weeping of his young wife seemed meaningless. 'I would have stayed with you, if I had known that our life together was to be so short! Why did you let me go?'

Tragedies were not only happening to the young, like Thu Lan and her husband, but also to the old who had been left alone to witness the fall of the younger generation. I could not hold back my tears as I repeated these moving words from a south Vietnamese folk song that was popular during the war:

> *Giot mua tren la nuoc mat me gia*
> *la cha dam dia tren xac con lanh gia. . .*
> The rain on the leaves is the bitter tears
> of a mother who hears her son is no more. . .

My aunt Thuyen faced tragedy in the vast empty airforce reception hall of Saigon's Tan Son Nhat Airport. A row of coffins lay in line and were honoured with flags and wreaths. The coffins contained the bodies of the airforce crews who were killed while on mission — and one of them, she was told, belonged to her. It was no different from the others. All were closed and sealed. But the heartbroken mother believed it — that was it. That was the end of everything. The end of a son she had loved and treasured, of one on whom she had leant for protection since her husband had left her for another woman. But most of all, it was the end point of her great fear, the fear of losing a son in war!

'Why did you go, my son? You said it was not your mission.' The suspicion that surrounded that fatal assignment which caused the sudden death of my cousin Tuan — a trustworthy young man in his early thirties, and a pilot in the VNAF (the South Vietnamese Airforce) — has remained a mystery!

A week after the funeral, when we had thought the tragedy was over, a group of high ranking military officers, both Vietnamese and American, appeared at my aunt Thuyen's home and courteously asked Tuan's mother for a special permit to dig up her son's new grave just for a quick investigation of the body. 'We just want to look for a small detail, that's all!'

'That's all? What else do you want to do to a dead person in the grave? No, no! I'm not going to let you! Everything is over!'

'Please, Mrs Thuyen! We would like your kind co-operation, but we're afraid we will have to do it with or without your consent!'

Tuan's family was denied permission to be present at the exhumation. Mac Dinh Chi was a large ancient cemetery built by the French and located in the middle of Saigon. Opposite the lengthy lofty ancient wall of the cemetery was a busy street. Tuan's family was determined to find their own way to watch the exhumation set at midnight the next day. They arranged with a family living in a three-storey terrace house right opposite the cemetery to allow them to watch from the top of their building. From there the family used a pair of binoculars and followed every move.

In the still silence of the cemetery and the darkness of the night, a dark green ambulance and a military police jeep turned in at the cemetery gate. Both cars ran along the inside road, then stopped at the new grave. Five men in plain military uniforms got out of the ambulance. The headlights from the police car suddenly broke through the darkness and illuminated the grave. The digging began. About fifteen minutes later, the coffin could be seen. Tuan's family watched every single move. The coffin was opened. There was no investigation. A plastic bag — the size of a person — was taken out of the grave and carried to the ambulance and a similar bag was taken quickly from the ambulance and put into the coffin. Everything was then put back into place.

The next morning, the family found the white headband of mourning lying on the ground. Traditionally, the white band is placed around the head of the coffin if the person happens to die before the parents. But the Americans did not understand this tradition.

Tuan's gravestone has never yet borne his name. The family does not believe it is Tuan's resting place.

Why did those military officers not tell the truth to Tuan's family? What did they do to the dead body from Tuan's grave? Why were those American officers involved in this matter at all? Was Tuan's body swapped for a missing American because Tuan was tall and well built? Or was an American body misplaced and given to Tuan's family?

Since then, rightly or wrongly, a fresh fragrant bouquet of flowers has been placed by Tuan's family each year on the grave. Even though the bouquet may be for the unknown, it was still blood shed for this suffering land.

8

Warnings of impending doom: March – April 1975

ONE AFTERNOON IN EARLY MARCH 1975, we were gathered in the living room of my home in one of Saigon's busiest suburbs. All of us were watching the news on television anxiously. The news reader was speaking frantically about the Vietnamese communist forces who were attacking the provincial cities and towns of central Vietnam. Streams of refugees were fleeing south.

Cuu Nuoc la yeu Nuoc, 'To save our country is to love our country'; *Chong Cong la luat cuu Nuoc*, 'Fighting against the communist is the key act in saving our country'. These slogans and more appeared constantly on television from President Thieu to his army. He pleaded to his troops to try their best to battle against the Viet Cong 'with the last drop of our blood to preserve the freedom of the south'.

A few days earlier, Tuyet — my eldest sister — left her home in Dalat, fleeing to Saigon with her four children. An urgent evacuation order by the authorities was secretly given to all the military families in central Vietnam to move to a safer area. But all military men had to remain at their military posts. Tran was one of them.

Tuyet and the children arrived at my home exhausted. She told us of her tragic flight. Dalat is about 300 kilometres north of Saigon. Though it was a beautiful, wealthy town, everything in Dalat was limited. Its small population meant there was only one commercial flight a day from Saigon.

That day, the number of passengers trying to fly to Saigon was overwhelming. People had suddenly left every-thing — family houses and treasured possessions — determined to get to Saigon at any cost. It did not matter if the plane was overloaded. People fought for a space, not necessarily a seat, with or without a ticket.

'We were all terrified of being left and being taken by the Viet Cong,' Tuyet said. 'The whole situation was chaotic. I thought we would never get on the flight, though the tickets were in our hands. Then a male crew member intervened on behalf of the legitimate passengers. He took a risk, but pulled each of my children from the lift where they were stuck among those without tickets. He pulled them in like heavy pieces of luggage. Otherwise I could not have got them. We were lucky to get inside before the plane actually took off.'

Why did people have to leave this place in such a hurry? Nobody seemed to know and be prepared to talk about it; yet all were doing the same thing! Inside the plane, in a suffocating state, a strange silence existed among the passengers.

In fact people were vaguely aware of the rapid advance of the communists. But little did we believe it was any-thing more severe than that the territory which belonged to the Republic of Vietnam would be tragically reduced.

*   *   *

Luat, one of my cousins, swept into my home like a strong gust of wind. He parked his motorbike along the veranda, rushed inside, closed the door and came straight to the room where we were sitting.

'Sisters! Turn off the TV!' Luat looked serious. He

lowered his voice. 'I have important news to tell you!'

'What is it? What is it?' We all stared at him surprised.

'I'm supposed not to tell you the source of this information; but this news is really true. I do hope you all believe me, sisters!'

We all looked at him puzzled. Luat, in a very emotional voice, articulated each word slowly and clearly. 'Believe it or not, Saigon will be handed over to the Viet Cong within one month!'

'You must be joking!'

'No, I'm not joking. I'm telling you the truth.'

'It's impossible! Tran's still posted in Dalat. If it were so, he would have let us know!'

'It doesn't matter any more whether he's here or in Dalat. We'll soon all be ruled by the Viet Cong!'

Tuyet recalled the situation in Dalat just a few days ago, then said, 'Why didn't Tran say a word about it? He's a military man — he should have known about it. No, I don't think so. It might be just another Tet Offensive like in 1968. Can you tell me who told you this news?'

'No I can't. But it's true and serious, sister!'

'Do you mean *Viet nam Cong Hoa* (the Republic of Vietnam) has failed? No, it couldn't have. Everything depends on America; and they've never failed!'

'Please believe me. Do try your best to leave Vietnam as soon as possible, otherwise you will regret it. I'm trying too for my own family. We really don't have much time!'

Luat is the son of my Aunt Sa, my mother's twin sister. He had a young wife and two small children. He had a military position in Saigon, and was also a university student. I looked at Luat and knew he had tried his best to convince us that what he had said was really true.

'But how do we get out of the country? I've got no idea at all,' I said.

Worried and anxious, Luat whispered, 'Honestly, I don't know how yet. . . even for my own family. But we've got to try hard and find out. There must be a way. I pray we'll meet together again outside of Vietnam; otherwise the only other place is in heaven! I'm serious!'

Luat shook hands with each of us and murmured, '. . . in America! . . .in America!' The farewell sounded funny; yet it conveyed an eager wish like the last words written in a will. He rushed outside, then hopped on his motor-bike. As he left, Luat shouted back into the house, 'I'll catch up with you all next week!' — appearing to want to divert any possible suspicion on the part of our neighbours.

The whole thing seemed so strange. It was like an act in a badly written comedy in which Luat had just completed the rehearsal. It was ridiculous, and did not make any sense. However, we were anxious to know what other people thought, particularly Tran, to see if he could explain Luat's news. Meanwhile our only immediate worry was Tran's situation in Dalat.

A few days after this, my office director — a Canadian man in his mid-thirties — held a meeting with all the office staff. And nothing was more ridiculous than what we heard from him that day. 'As our work is lessening every day, we'd like to encourage each of you to feel free to look for another job at another place.'

'What! How? Why?' the staff noisily commented. Yet no further satisfactory explanation was given.

The director, in a futile effort to compensate with some kindness, added, 'Our office will support each of you — if you plan to leave — by giving you three months' wages.'

'What the hell can we do, friends?' Sanh, a normally quiet person, cried out. 'Only crazy people would ask staff to leave a permanent job for a nowhere job!' Another laughed, 'Go ahead, Sanny! It's great to have three months

doing nothing! Then come back! I'll employ you again!'
The joke fell flat.

After the meeting, a heavy atmosphere smothered the
usual friendliness in the office. I wondered whether anybody at work knew about the expected collapse of the
south and the takeover by the Viet Cong.

As the fierce fighting in central Vietnam reached its
peak, we prayed desperately and waited for Tran. He was
the only family member whose military duty had held him
in Dalat.

Although my small house was overcrowded with family members in the heat, I enjoyed the presence of my eldest
sister's family, an opportunity which we usually had only
once a year. We all thought this disturbance was temporary, and soon everybody would be back in their own
place.

In mid-March, Tran suddenly turned up in Saigon, terrified and bewildered. He and thousands of other military
men of the ARVN troops were unexpectedly ordered to
withdraw from all northern provinces of south Vietnam,
including Dalat. Tran recalled that after the shock of the
secret order to succumb to the enemy, Tran had quietly left
his Dalat home in his jeep to head for Nha Trang. Unbeknown to him, this was the end of his happy life. The
endless national highway heading south was flooded with
countless refugees and military men who challenged death
to flee south. At great cost they faced danger from the Viet
Cong.

There were no evacuation channels to support the
refugees or the ARVN men who had stood firm defending
the country against the enemy. The call from their com-
mander-in-chief, Mr Thieu, had created utter chaos and
totally demoralised the army. When a noisy old motorised
pedicab finally stopped in front of my house at 7.30 p.m.

that evening to let Tran out, he was greeted by all of us as a hero for surviving another battle. We were overjoyed. It was risky and frightening; but it was over. Everybody thought it was just another battle against the Viet Cong; now it was over. And the south — the actual southern Vietnamese territory — was still believed to be a safe refuge for those who had never wished to surrender their freedom. It had, after all, become a refuge for almost a million northern Vietnamese since the Geneva Accords were signed in 1954 — surely it was safe!

My office was situated in the heart of Saigon in an area which included a number of foreign embassies. As one of thousands of people living in the city, I had never actually witnessed the 'real' war, but the acts of terrorism which happened around towns and cities, such as bombings or plastic explosives hidden underneath the public transport vehicles, in front of embassies, in cinemas, restaurants, night-clubs and at countless other places, made life wretched. In a moment a lively night-club could be turned into a seething mass of blood and flesh. Most terrifying of all was that this kind of battle was always led by 'ghost soldiers' and at any time and place so that people could not predict what might happen.

But the American Embassy building somehow gave us an impression of steadfastness. I met a friend who was a high school teacher. His parents had fled south from Hanoi in 1954, and over a cup of coffee I asked him if he knew the truth about the reported American withdrawal.

'Can you see that over there?' He turned to the US Embassy building. 'They're still there and working. I don't believe the Americans will withdraw. They've never failed in the past. At the very least they must have a fair plan worked out for both sides.'

'But I believe since the French left, the war in our

country has become a kind of civil war. Perhaps America doesn't want to be involved in it any longer.'

'Personally, I think world wars or civil wars, conquests or invasions are outdated; it's time for people to understand the common principles of freedom and stand together for what is right.'

In early April, the reported withdrawal became an open secret. Yet it was only talked about in private with close trusted friends and family. Those who knew the actual source of the secret took it seriously; others could not believe it.

One afternoon at about 2.00 p.m., when the heat was as always overwhelming, Ngoc glanced from her desk to mine and said, 'How about an iced white strong coffee, Phuong?' A glass of strong freshly brewed coffee mixed with condensed milk and crushed ice would be perfect.

Ngoc was a small attractive young woman in her early twenties. She had been working with me for about two years. She was married to the son of a well-known church minister in Saigon, and had just had a baby, now about six months old. Her young husband, a university student, had been drafted into the army, and was a second lieutenant posted in Vung Tau, a small coastal town about 100 kilometres east of Saigon.

Ngoc, not waiting for my answer, went quickly to the front desk where she would telephone our canteen to order our coffee.

'Excuse me, Phuong.' A soft male voice spoke from behind me. I looked back and saw Tung. 'May I see Ngoc for a minute please?'

'Ngoc has just gone to the canteen. She'll be back in a minute,' I told Tung. 'Anything I can do for you now?'

Tung did not seem in a hurry, but also did not intend to wait for Ngoc. He handed something to me wrapped in an old white handkerchief. 'Yes, please give this to

Ngoc. It's from her mother-in-law. That's all. I don't really need to see her.'

Tung thanked me and disappeared down the winding staircase from our second floor. Ngoc came back and I gave her the package. 'What is it? From my mother-in-law?' Ngoc's face changed colour quickly. She almost jerked the thing out of my hand and opened it, shaking. Inside another paper wrapping were some heavy items of gold jewellery with a handwritten note:

Dear Ngoc,
We're so sorry, but we have to leave you. Here is
some jewellery for you in case you need it.
We're praying for you.

Mother-in-law

Ngoc burst into tears. All the staff in my department came over. We surrounded Ngoc, stared at the note and tried to understand what it really meant. The note sounded so simple, but Ngoc, though she was in shock and still crying, showed that there was something more behind it. She did not intend to tell us, but was determined to leave work immediately.

She went home, took her baby boy with her and went straight to Vung Tau to see her husband. Nobody in the office cared about work any more for the rest of that afternoon. We were so confused and tried to find out what the significance of the note was. I thought that it might relate to what my cousin Luat had said to my family about the Viet Cong takeover and the need to leave. After work I rushed home and told my family what had happened in our office.

The next morning all Saigon newspapers carried headlines which shocked everybody. An aircraft had been hijacked by some Vietnamese pilots and flown across the sea to Singapore. At first the plane was not allowed to land in Singapore. But after a few hours of circling illegally in the air, the Singapore government allowed it to land. I was astonished that the flight carried a group of people whom I knew very well. It was Ngoc's in-laws and their wealthy friends and families, including the family of a church minister who had been leading a large congregation. They were actually given the status of refugees escaping from the communist takeover of the south.

Two of Ngoc's in-laws were pilots in the airforce. They had secretly assembled selected family and friends near Saigon, then captured the aircraft and flown to Singapore. Ngoc was also supposed to be included in the escape with her husband and their little boy. But the ARVN troops were still applying strict control on troop movements, and Khang — like thousands of other army people — was not able to obtain a travel permit from his commander to return to Saigon.

We noticed an increased number of Vietnamese police around the US Embassy building. This was unusual. Many Vietnamese, mostly women and children, gathered quietly in front of the embassy each day. They waited all day for something. We all wondered who they were and what they were doing there.

Shortly after the hijack, our office staff were ordered to remove all our name plaques on our desks and destroy all computer print-out lists of names and addresses of our overseas supporters. Our office was the field office of one of the world's largest private voluntary organisations.

The fate of the south by this time was no more in doubt. Living under communism threatened us all. The pressing issue was how to avoid them, how to get away from them! Yet we were groping as if blindfolded.

We heard that the US Embassy had been organising for US citizens, their Vietnamese employees, and the Vietnamese who were married to Americans to leave Saigon. They would also help to evacuate the Vietnamese who could prove they had connections with the Americans, such as those working for foreign organisations and agencies.

We were also told that all foreigners' offices could issue name lists of their Vietnamese staff signed by the actual foreign boss; this would permit those Vietnamese people to pass through the Tan Son Nhat Airport checkpoint to get on any evacuation planes leaving Saigon. All these people would certainly be victims of the communist government. But we also heard that any moves to leave were considered by the Vietnamese authorities as treasonous. Little did we realise that in those turbulent days there was no law; even the leader of the nation was preparing his own escape.

In our own office, we had not heard about the evacuation organised for the staff by our director and his Vietnamese executive assistant. The office was thought of as an organisation run by the Americans. We were frightened we would be the subjects of communist persecution. We believed an evacuation should have been arranged for us. We waited for the director to organise our evacuation, but we saw no sign of him and heard nothing from him.

My parents were given a more responsible position in the church and moved to a province in the Mekong delta. The close bonds of my large family — some were married and lived in different places — had made any plans for evacuation extremely difficult. When any opportunity appeared, we were uncertain if it would be possible to include all of them. We all were tortured by the thought of leaving the others to the sufferings which were coming.

Tran — my eldest sister's husband — believed strongly

he was subject to the ARVN authorities. He did not think he should make any arrangement to leave Saigon by road because he might be arrested as a deserter. Tran told me, 'I believe sooner or later your office will issue a staff name list. I'm sure — like other American organisations — the staff families will be included. I think my family and I would rather wait for you than try to go to Can Tho to join my brother.' Tran's brother was an army major; he had also been trying to arrange for his family's secret evacuation.

'But nobody has seen the director at all during these past few days,' I answered my brother-in-law. 'The office without a boss is a mess at the moment. I don't know for sure who has been taking responsibility for helping the staff!'

My parents knew about the evacuation of Tuyet's family from Dalat. They were concerned for them. But we had not heard whether or not they knew about the chaotic situation in Saigon. We decided to telephone them from Saigon, but we felt it dangerous to tell them over the phone what the problem was.

The next day my parents turned up from their province by the early morning bus. They obviously knew nothing about the sudden chaos in Saigon. At first my parents were shocked to see, hear and sense the uptight spirit of the people around and in my home. They were startled about our plan for the entire family to leave Vietnam.

'It's not true!' my father said. 'I've never believed in rumours!'

'But it's not a rumour, Papa. Things which have been happening all around prove it,' we said to my father.

'Tran is here. The ARVN troops from the central areas succumbed,' Tuyet added.

'We've been in this war for twenty years, but nothing like this has happened before,' I said.

'I believe time is not yet ready for the communists,' my father replied.

'But why, Papa?' In truth, we all were so anxious to hear something, anything that could prove the communists were not coming to the south. We had never wanted to leave our country.

'I believe only when the seeds of the good news are sown throughout the world that the communists will win. Even in our small country, not everyone has heard about our good news!'

I did not know whether or not my father was right, but this calmed us down amidst the city's feverish restless atmosphere. The next morning my parents left us to go back to the province.

I came to the office next day. Some people did not show up to work. A girlfriend at work received legal sponsorship papers from her overseas relatives to leave Vietnam. During the day, we heard the sound of helicopters landing and taking off from the top of the US Embassy building. I returned home from work feeling numb and so despondent.

Our front room was packed with people, relatives and friends who were visiting Tuyet and Tran and their children. Their talk was how to leave Saigon. From the middle room I heard my two brothers arguing over whether to leave the country, possibly forever. One definitely would not leave without our parents and our youngest brother. We also did not know how our other married sisters and their families were. We had not yet found any source of help, but we were preparing ourselves for a sudden rescue, especially at night time.

That evening Mrs Toan our neighbour visited my sister Tram and me. She was the wife of a military major. She said, 'Why don't you try hard to leave as soon as possible? I heard that the Viet Cong authorities will force southern single women to marry their disabled soldiers as a reward for their sacrifice to the country.'

Shocked by this horrible news, I said to Mrs Toan, 'I'd rather kill myself than let them hurt me in that way. I will, if I am faced with that situation!' When I recall this day, I now wonder if Mrs Toan really wanted to express her secret invitation to me and Tram to join her family's personal evacuation. But we did not understand her. Anyhow, Tram and I had never wished to make any attempt to escape without the members of our family. Two days later we were shocked to know that Mrs Toan and her family had gone secretly. They left everything in their house untouched, just as if it were still occupied normally.

'Unbelievable!' Tran, though worried and depressed, could not suppress his ever-present sense of humour. 'This is exactly how the "second coming" will be! I just talked with him at church yesterday. This morning I went to his home and his house was empty. He and his whole family had gone!'

'How do you know they've gone?' Tuyet asked.

'The neighbour said she heard the unusual sound of a car stop at about 2.00 a.m. this morning to pick up the family. She guessed that's what it was.' Tuyet was not amused by her husband's thought.

Rumours of the compulsory marriages to the Viet Cong disabled soldiers spread around the city quickly. I heard that amidst the turmoil there were at least three engaged couples in our church community who decided to get married in a collective wedding service without concern for traditions. There was only a get-together for a special prayer and for the lawful papers to be issued for them as husbands and wives.

One afternoon I happened to see Al, an American, who had left Phnom Penh just before the takeover of Cambodia by the Khmer Rouge. I did not know much about Al except that he was a member of our international organisation based in Cambodia and he only knew me as a person who was working in this office. However, I felt I was drowning. If there was no actual buoy for me then I must lean on a piece of driftwood. I followed Al into the office and asked him for help to get through the airport checkpoint. Al seemed concerned. He said, 'I'll try to see if I can help you.'

'Al, I understand it's got really nothing to do with you, but would you please be kind enough to help my family, too?' It took all my courage to ask this.

'How many people are in your family?' Al asked.

'Around twelve. I know it's not a small number of people. But I beg you, please help!'

'I'm so sorry, Phuong. I'll try to help you, because I know you're part of this office, but that's all I can do.'

'I'm not married. My brothers and sisters are my family. Please help. I can't go without them!' I repeated the same thing again and again; but Al only agreed to help if I was prepared to leave by myself.

I felt time was running out. In bed that night I sobbed my heart out. The more the planes roared overhead at night, the more people I knew would be gone the next day.

About mid-April we were shocked when word came that the director had just left Saigon. The hope of an evacuation all of a sudden evaporated. Instead, we heard that Thinh, one of the staff members, had the evacuation permit in his hands. Thinh had been working at this office for a few years and he had not been considered a trustworthy person by most of the staff. All my friends and I at first hoped that our overwhelming need to flee the communists would encourage him to fulfil his responsibilities as honestly as possible. For a few days there was at least hope again in my family.

My parents were concerned for our situation in Saigon; they visited us again. And again they were startled to see the unbelievable chaos of the city. Nevertheless my parents had decided, rightly or wrongly, to stay in Vietnam. In fact my mother, though confused over the tragedy which was unfolding and which might tear her family apart, had supported our idea of leaving if it was our choice. On the other hand my father, a sentimental person at heart, had been tortured by the thought that he would never see his children again! My father left for the province with the hope that somehow he would still see us again. My mother decided to stay with us until the day we would leave Saigon.

Saigon now had taken on a messy, desolate appearance. Tram and I walked through the small arcade of Crystal Palace, a mini-luxurious shopping centre not far from Saigon central market. The music from a small kiosk, where cassette tapes of recorded music and songs were available for sale, resounded: *'Saigon dep lam! Saigon oi, Saigon oi! La la la la la!!'*, 'Saigon! Saigon! You are so beautiful!' Those words from a very popular song sung by many, even by some Americans who used to enjoy some good aspects of the once beautiful city, suddenly struck me as bitter and mocking.

I felt confused, frightened and restless. I said to Tram, 'I'm afraid we're taking a risk leaving Saigon, and not knowing whether other people will accept us or not.'

'It's a risk whether we stay or we leave. But to me it's better to take the risk of going,' Tram answered.

'Why are you so sure about it? Yesterday I talked with Khanh about the idea of leaving. When she told her husband what I had said he disagreed with me and seemed rather annoyed.'

'What did he say?'

'"Other people can live; why can't we? It depends on our positive attitude." He doesn't seem desperate at all!'

'That's just his idea,' Tram said firmly. 'We must not be diverted by such arguments.'

Shortly after I arrived home that afternoon, the mother of Minh Hang, a friend I had worked with, came to see me. Hang had left Saigon for the US to further her education and had decided to stay there permanently.

'I'm so glad to see you; but what brings you here, dear Aunt?' I asked her. Customarily, people always call parents of close friends uncle and aunt.

'I've tried my best, but until now I've not seen any opportunity for me and my family to leave Vietnam. That's why I came to see you.'

She handed me a long letter which she had written to her daughter, and said, 'Phuong, I'm sure you will leave soon through your organisation. I've always felt you were a trusted friend of Minh Hang. The last favour I'd like to ask is that you will give this letter to Hang once you get out of Vietnam. I may not be able to see her for the rest of my life. Please tell her that I've loved her and I always will.'

I could not hold back my tears after those emotional words. I took the letter from her and said, 'My office is a mess. The boss has gone. I'm not sure whether I will be able to get out or not. But if I do, I'm sure I will find her for you.' We said goodbye in tears.

While I was talking with Hang's mother, another friend came to see my brother-in-law. He was a student at theological college. He admitted he was greatly disappointed at seeing the pastor, his most trusted spiritual model, had quietly left the country, relinquishing his role as a shepherd without a hint at this most turbulent time of faith. Truly, most people were wrapped in a dark cloud of despair.

Saigon was by this time on full alert. Hundreds of unknown people wormed their way into our office compound by night, waiting for a chance to escape. Several employees who were single or with small families left their homes and hid themselves in the office building hoping for a miracle at night. In front of the embassy building, there were thousands of people making desperate efforts to get into the American Embassy for a flight to freedom.

A few days had passed since Thinh told everybody that he was organising the official evacuation for our office staff. Nothing had happened. Instead, we heard that he had been using the official permits to organise transport for people outside the office in order to make money for himself.

People were bewildered by the shock resignation of Mr Nguyen Van Thieu, the president of south Vietnam, viewed on television. It was 21 April 1975. I rushed to my office the following morning to see what the evacuation situation was. This, coupled with the news of Thinh's treachery, struck me speechless. All hope and expectation suddenly evaporated.

'We've been foolish to put all our eggs in one rotten basket!' a staff member shouted angrily.

'There's no time for regrets. Let's work our own way out together,' another said. The following day, we decided to use blank personnel ID cards and type in the names of each staff member. These cards were actually required for staff who had to travel for their work. However, we soon realised that we were not able to have the actual signature of our boss on the cards, and this would make the cards useless. Should we forge the boss's unique tangled signature on the ID cards? A dreadful argument broke out among close friends. Who would be able to imitate the signature and who would be willing to be responsible for this kind of action? The whole world was collapsing in front of my eyes.

The sounds of the evacuation helicopters continued whirring atop the embassy building, and on some other apartment buildings around the city. All of a sudden, a crack, a gunshot was heard inside our office compound, near the warehouse. Terrified, we rushed out to see what was happening. Several more gunshots were fired by an angry depressed soldier who had hidden in our compound for the last few days, hoping to 'hitchhike' to freedom.

My friends and I dropped everything and ran to the front gate in order to get out of the compound before he tried anything worse. The front gate was locked. We turned around and rushed to the back. We helped each other climb over the high fence which divided our office building and the other. I squeezed between the fence bars. We spilt out onto the street, said goodbye to each other, and scattered.

On the evening of April 28, my brothers said, 'The Vietcong army troops are sure to move into Saigon city tomorrow or the next day.' Most terrifying of all, their route of entry was to be near our home.

Navy personnel had left the city with their families on their ships. Many went to Bach Dang harbour, trying to jump on any ship available. We longed to be among those lucky people. But we were too far away from the harbour, and were cut off by a military checkpoint. Even at this stage evacuations from our area were still restricted by the local authority.

Further, we would risk losing our family house if we all left home and the attempt was unsuccessful, and we tried to come back.

There were many desperate stories. Some people accidentally missed the secret evacuation at the last minute. Some mysteriously disappeared, leaving their families, wives and children in a state of terror. Some threw themselves on board and suddenly the ship left the dock to escape the disruption of the port security, leaving other family members still on the wharf under a shower of gunshots from security police.

My mother was at home with Tuyet's children. She went to market, cooked, washed and cleaned. She did everything with tremendous patience and love, hoping we would eventually find our way to freedom and happiness. 'Mama, we think you should go back to Papa before we run away from this place,' Tuyet told my mother with a broken heart.

'No, I will not leave you until you all go,' my mother said firmly.

Early the following morning — 29 April — we separated and walked cautiously through the military checkpoint guarding the area in which we lived, trying to be as normal as possible, like people who were going for a small thing to the market. My brothers and brother-in-law had already made their way out on their motorbikes and bicycles. Once we had passed our busy shopping area, we planned to take a taxi to Saigon harbour.

Imagine our shock when we reached the main streets and found thousands of people running from our area towards the city. Frightened, my mother asked a passing woman what was happening.

'Viet Cong! Viet Cong are coming in! This way! This way!' the terrified woman replied, looking back.

Several men dashed by on motorbikes shouting to other people running along the street, 'Hurry up! Hurry up! They are armed and will kill us!'

Tuyet and Tram pulled my mother's arm to cross the

street. There was no public transport. People were colliding with each other, totally confused. My mother was
about to collapse. Her knees knocked together.

'Oh God! Cyclo, cyclo! Please stop!' Tram happened
to have caught a cyclo rushing by. The cyclo driver
stopped. 'Mama, you must go on a cyclo. Otherwise
you'll collapse soon!' Tram urged my mother.

'But where am I going to?' my mother asked, hopping
on the cyclo. 'Back to our house?'

'Oh no! They won't let you in at the moment! Go to
Pastor Ba's. Pastor Ba's church, Mama! Can you hear me?
We'll meet you there soon,' Tuyet said trembling. I do not
know how Tuyet got the idea of going to this church. But
it was our best hope.

Our plan to go to the harbour was abandoned. After
my mother had taken the only cyclo seen on the whole
street, we ran until we reached the church which was about
twenty kilometres from our home.

My whole family met there. There were at least thirty
people packed in a small room in the upstairs part of the
church building. We did not know each other, but the
pastor and his wife knew us all. Like us, most of them
were from different churches. Around Saigon were some
who had been evacuated from central Vietnam. We did not
understand why we ended up in this place; but nobody
bothered to talk or ask. Our dilemma was enough to think
about.

Each family group sat on the floor quietly, as if we could
hide ourselves forever from the enemy. I thought of my
house, wondering how it was at the moment. Had the Viet
Cong actually got there? How were my other married
sisters and their families? Had they gone? How was my
father by himself down in the province?

Later that evening, a young woman's cry broke the

quietness of the night. Her husband — a navy captain — had gone with his ship. After several unsuccessful attempts to evacuate his wife and their two small children, he was gone. His life would have been at risk had he stayed. Our hearts went out to this young wife. Then in the far corner of the room another young woman started to sob. And before we realised what was upsetting her, the young husband suddenly stood straight up, and pulled a pistol from his trousers pocket!

'Oh please, friend, don't!' one of the men said in a gentle voice.

'Oh God! My position is hopeless!' he uttered. 'I'm a pilot! I should have flown away with my family. It's too late now! Too late!' He collapsed and dropped the gun on the floor. 'Why didn't God help me? Why?'

Everybody woke up in the quiet, heavy atmosphere of the room early the next morning. It was a little after 6.00 a.m. All the men, including my brothers, were out of the room on the street. What was going to happen today? My brothers and some other men suddenly stormed back into the room. 'Listen, everybody! It's over! Everything is over. Viet Cong are already right here!'

It was like a bolt from the blue! Everybody sat on the floor speechless, numb, as if unconscious.

Suddenly Bao, one of my brothers, took hold of his dog tag worn around his neck and screamed out, 'No more! No more is Bao a soldier of *Viet Nam Cong Hoa!*' He yanked at the tag, broke it and smashed the pieces bearing his name, his blood group and his military service number in his hand. And he cried copiously like a little child.

It was 30 April 1975.

9

The blood-red flag:
May – December, 1975

I SHOOK MY HEAD, rubbing my eyes harder and harder.
Then I opened my eyes again. I still saw the same thing. It
was enormous, red, a terrifying drastic red. It hung on the
opposite house. The colour filled the frame of my front room
window. The strong piercing red, reflected in the morning
rays of the sun, was like a pool of blood.

My eyes focussed on the middle of the red and saw the
shape of a star, a huge yellow star wriggling in the breeze.
It looked like a star of fate floundering before falling. 'Oh
God!' I uttered painfully, burying my face in my trembling
hands. 'It's the Viet Cong flag! It's true! It's not an April
nightmare any more! It's here and it's reality!'

I burst into tears. My heart ached as if its flesh was
actually torn by sharp claws. My spirit hurt so much that
I thought only death would accommodate my feelings.
'Vietcong! Go away! I don't need you here!' I shouted
painfully into the silence of my mind. 'I've got to finish
that memo at work. . . My boss wants a report from me
next week. . . Is my new dress ready for me to pick up?
I've got to go to a wedding this weekend. . . I must do the
washing today!'

I repeated these phrases over and over; they were part

of my life. They sounded absolutely normal and reasonable.

Today's reality was unquestionably abnormal. Why don't I go to work and just sit there like a loafer? This is not normal! Why are Tuyet and her family here while they should be at home in Dalat? This is not normal! Why are Bao and Anh — my two soldier brothers — here while they should be at their military posts? This is not normal! It is not Christmas or Tet, but they all are here doing nothing! People should be at work or at school at this time of the day, but they are all here wondering what the future will be.

'Ho Chi Minh Muon Nam! Ho Chi Minh Muon Nam!', 'Long Live Ho Chi Minh! Long live Ho Chi Minh!' A group of small children in their school uniforms — blue shorts, white shirt and red scarf — led by a ferocious-looking teenager passed my house. They cheerfully shouted the number one slogan of the Vietnamese communists. Their tiny fists went up and down in time with their shouts.

The sounds brought me in touch with reality. Viet Cong! They represented in the minds of most southerners cruelty, inhumanity, vengefulness and death. And now all of a sudden Viet Cong were everywhere in the city — on the streets, in the markets, in the shops, on the buses. They walked side by side with Saigon people! A chill ran down my spine.

After the first shock on the morning of 30 April 1975, my brothers rushed back to our home area by a circuitous route not yet controlled by the 'liberation' forces. Obeying the first official announcement heard everywhere, my brothers bought a communist flag — a yellow star based on red — to stick on the front of our house, so that it would be recognised as rightfully occupied. Otherwise it could be seized and confiscated by the new power. The flags miraculously appeared for sale everywhere. We returned to our home during the morning, exhausted and depressed!

My mother decided that we — all the women and children — must go with her to the province for a special break, to relieve some of the tension and strain of the last two months, no matter what tomorrow would bring. The men of the family, however, were to stay in Saigon to keep our house occupied and safe. As members of the former regime, especially those who had been in the army, they awaited their fate nervously.

On 1 May 1975, two days after the takeover, although it was very early, we left Saigon for our province. When the bus entered the main road of the town where we were to change buses, the sight was poignant. Countless used military uniforms, boots, helmets and other war materials were along the road, at the marketplace — everywhere. Later we found out that until the previous day, thousands of ARVN troops posted in remote areas and jungles of the Mekong delta were not aware of events in Saigon. Soldiers from some areas were not even aware of the earlier resignation of President Thieu.

When the surrender of General Duong Van Minh — the new president — was announced, they dragged themselves out of their military posts in the jungles and small towns and disarmed themselves in great fear of being recognised as ARVN soldiers by their enemies. All of a sudden the enemy had become their ruler.

We changed buses. Now the bus was packed with people — civilians and ex-soldiers — sitting and standing all over the place. They looked bewildered and in tatters. A kind man gave up his seat for my mother. Everybody was talking.

'What the hell did he do to his people?' A man was very angry. He meant President Thieu. 'We listened to his appeal! We meant to fight until the "last drop of blood" as he asked us to. Even yesterday in the jungle, my commanding officer still led us effectively in our defence!'

A young man, apparently more resentful, said, 'ARVN soldiers were strong enough if the "big man" hadn't surrendered! Remember the Tet Offensive? American soldiers did not help my company at that time, but we won!'

Others seemed to face a different dilemma.

'We had to leave school early before having a career in order to become soldiers to fight for peace. Now all of a sudden the peace comes from the other direction! We have no peacetime career,' said a middle-aged man.

'I'm glad there'll be no more fighting! I have an only girl. She's married to a soldier. I was in constant fear for his safety. And instead of their looking after me, I had to work hard to help his wife and their two little children. Now he doesn't have to fight anymore,' an old woman explained.

'At least I can go back to what I really am. A carpenter. For many years my hands were used only for shooting,' a young man said.

But I felt tired and sick. The noisy talking, the raucous laughter, the heavy, stinking atmosphere in the bus with the growing heat, all overwhelmed me. It was about another fifteen kilometres before we would reach the ferry to cross a large river. Suddenly all the buses stopped and the passengers were requested to get off. The drivers refused to continue the trip as they normally did. Instead, they returned to Saigon in order to make more trips and make more money.

It was then that I noticed thousands of people — men, women, children — with piles of luggage all heading for the ferry. Motorbikes and some private cars full of people moved slowly along the road jammed with walking and running people. It was chaotic. Who were all these people? Where were they going? We did not understand. But at that moment we just did not bother about it.

The fifteen-kilometre walk to the ferry exhausted my mother and my nieces in particular. 'Maybe we'll have to be impolite and ask for a ride in a private car,' I said to Tuyet and Tram. My sisters seemed uncertain; but I felt oppressed by the heat. I did not wait for them to agree. I saw in one car only two young men. They looked pleasant and their car was moving slowly. I grasped the opportunity.

'Excuse me!' I waved my hands to stop them. 'Please help my mother and our two girls, just to the ferry. They can't walk any more.'

The car stopped. The two men looked at us and at each other. Both were in their late twenties. The one who drove the car seemed pleasant and wanted to help; but the other looked unhappy and did not say a word. At that moment, I felt wretched. Never before had we not been able to care for ourselves and had to beg for help as we did now. And I just could not stop crying.

'Yes, please get in,' the pleasant man said happily, and hopped out of the car to open the back door for us.

'How many of you altogether, ma'am?' the man asked.

'We're four altogether and two little girls,' my mother said, pushing our nieces into the car.

'Oh, plenty of room in the back seat. Please all get in!' And he smiled. 'All small people. It doesn't hurt my car a bit.'

'How kind you are to us!' my mother said gratefully.

We all got in and felt how much we appreciated these people at that moment. But we were exhausted and our feelings were so low that we could not cope with talking any more. The two young men were no different. They were quiet and each seemed to be pursuing his own thoughts.

Suddenly the unhappy man broke the silence. 'I guess you're originally from Saigon, ma'am?'

'We're from the province. But most of our children are from Saigon. And one family from Dalat. How about yourselves? Are you from Saigon, too? Are you brothers?'

'No, ma'am. We're friends. We're from the navy and also from Saigon'.

'Is that so! My sons and son-in-law are from the army.'

I then felt like something had opened up between us and the two young men. There was no doubt that we were all in the same boat, people of an abandoned regime. The men told us they missed the evacuation on their ship from Saigon, and almost killed themselves for that. Now they were hoping to find their way out from Con Son Island before it too was taken over by the new power.

As they spoke, the burning desire to leave came back to us. Tuyet whispered to me and Tram, 'Do you think we should discuss it with them? Let Mama go back with Papa, and we'll all join them? I think she would be happy for us.' Momentarily, I thought this might be a wonderful chance for Tram and me as we did not have a family of our own.

'But they've already taken over!' Tuyet said, keeping her voice low.

'Yes. But they're not able to control the coastline and islands at the moment. Not yet. In fact their navy is terrible,' one of the men said.

'Is that why people are going in this direction?' Tram suddenly asked.

'I'm sure it is!' answered the other man.

The flow of people towards the ferry was so great that hours had already passed since we got in the car, but we had travelled nowhere. Apart from the public ferry boat that was jammed with people and heavy vehicles sluggishly travelling back and forth, quite a few small private boats were busy taking the overflow passengers across the large river. It was late in the afternoon. We thought we could not depend on this car any more, though the two kind men had promised us that once their car got across the river they would be happy to drive past our district. But they were on their way to escape. They could not afford to get stuck here for long and could not be expected to take us home if they continued to be delayed. They might have to abandon their car somewhere around here to take another route.

We decided to take the risk of going on one of those small private boats. It was quicker, but not always safe. We got out of the car and said goodbye in tearful silence, though we had met with each other for only a few hours. 'We'll think of you and God bless!' my mother said.

The unhappy man suddenly held my small niece in his hands and said in an emotional voice, 'I'll miss my little daughter. She's only a baby but beautiful, just like you!' He wiped his eyes.

'Why didn't you take your family with you?' Tuyet whispered.

'They're in another district. I had no time to arrange things for them.' Then he softened his voice. 'I had a top secret job in the navy. I'm in danger!'

The afternoon light faded quickly on the river. The breeze swept faintly over its surface, helping the overloaded boat packed with people, bicycles and all kinds of luggage on its way.

We finally reached our home at 8.00 p.m.

'Papa! Papa! Are you there?' We knocked at the door and shouted. 'We're here! Mama's here!'

'Oh God! You're still here? All of you?' My father

opened the door, sobbing with joy because we had not left the country.

Unlike the large towns in central Vietnam and Saigon itself, most of the south was still very quiet; people were not really aware of the traumatic events that had occurred in the past few months.

To our great surprise Van — my youngest sister — and her navy husband suddenly returned home. We had all believed they must have fled overseas. Unlike our critical situation in Saigon, they had plenty of opportunities to leave on warships, but their concern for their families had drawn them back.

After a week of rest, we left our parents to go back to the city, but we were confused and restless about the coming days. The appalling days of April were gone. Now it was time to wait for the new arrangements from the new authority.

Not long after returning to Saigon, Tuyet and Tran made plans to go back to their home in Dalat with their children. But word came from a relative that their home had been completely destroyed by the new local power soon after their evacuation to Saigon. The house was provided by the previous government for Tran and his family. To them, the house had been cherished.

They also heard that Viet Nam Thuong Tin, one of the Vietnamese commercial banks in Dalat, where they had a savings account, had been closed and the owners had fled the country. And so there was no way to get their money back.

And so we all squeezed into our tiny home in Saigon.

One morning amidst the devastation, Tran, depressed and nervous, pedalled into town to see the city's new face. It was scarred and tattered. Along some of the most popular and busy streets in the heart of Saigon, heaps of household goods and shop merchandise — new, used, unusual, expensive — were being sold at low prices. Browsing among the goods were some northern soldiers. A careful look revealed that the goods had been stolen from abandoned houses, shops and stores whose owners had fled the city.

On Le Loi Avenue, not far from the most popular city bookshop, Nha Sach Khai Tri, valuable books of all sorts and magazines were on sale at unbelievably low prices. Tran bought *The Gulag Archipelago*. Translated into French, it was in fact the poignant diary of a former high ranking artillery officer who had been one of thousands of victims in the communist brainwash camps of Russia. Tran came home, read it for three days — and was chilled!

For three days — 8, 9 and 10 May — all the ARVN troops, administrative officials and employees of foreign companies and organisations were requested to report to the revolutionary power at several different locations in Saigon and provincial cities.

'It's unbelievable!' Tran rushed home overjoyed. 'In fact it's wonderful!'

'Why are you so happy?' we asked, surprised.

'I'll be away from home for only ten days. Ten days being re-educated, in order to become a normal citizen. I think it's wonderful! I don't mind at all!' And he added, 'It's not at all like what I've read from that book I bought about being re-educated by the communists in Russia.'

And Tran, holding his wife and his children in his arms, said emotionally, 'After that we'll try to go back to Dalat and build our home again. What do you think, sweetheart?'

The new authorities also announced that everybody had to return to their own place for a population census. This was not just a count, but a check in order to establish clearly who was supposed to be in the urban areas and who was not, and what work they should be doing. It would also determine who had fled overseas.

Only with this announcement did people realise that they had never bothered to register before 'liberation'. People had lived where they wanted to in their own country; and did what they wished to do for a living. People also realised that evacuations and general chaos had created a situation that would be difficult to explain in a census.

Consequently we, along with countless others, had to beg the former local administrative officials who were being kept on the job to falsify the records for our safety. Eventually they registered my eldest sister's family and my two soldier brothers as permanent residents of our Saigon home. We were so relieved. But Tran met an ex-military friend who was originally from central Vietnam and had fled to Saigon with his family. When Tran asked him about his present situation in his area, he burst out, 'I wish I could kill them, *ba muoi thang tu*! My wife and I had to come to the district office and beg them from morning till evening for three days before they finally agreed to register my family members at the address where we are now!'

'But what does *ba muoi thang tu* mean? I've not heard it before,' Tran said.

'It's brand new slang. It means 'the thirtieth of April'. That's what people have started to call them, the former regime's people or officials who immediately — on 30 April — turned their backs on their brothers in order to make good their relationship with the new authority.'

Later these people were found all over the place and were considered dangerous. They spied on members of the former regime, reported falsely, or used personal evidence to blackmail them. People called them *'Dan 30'*, the 'thirtieth citizen'.

As the population census continued, hundreds of thousands of city people were forced to leave the city to *vung kinh te moi*, new economic zones.

'Do you know how I measured my hut?' The ex-soldier explained. 'I crawled into the middle of it, lay down and stretched out. My head was at the front door and my legs stuck out the back door. That's the size of the place I'm supposed to live in with my wife and my six children.'

His wife added tearfully, 'We'd tried hard to maintain this house for our family for many years. And now they claim it should belong to the authority, because my husband was a soldier. Our four children have been going to school here, and are suddenly taken away to live there and work in the fields. No education any more. I feel so terrible for my children'.

'What do people do for a living over there?' someone asked.

'Chop wood in the jungles. It's collective work for men and boys, from 5.30 a.m. to 6.30 p.m. each day. The local authority is the work controller and wood collector. Twenty per cent of the wood is left for the workers plus whatever food is grown by the families — women and children — with their bare hands on the untamed land.'

Back in the city, each family received an official family ration card issued by the district with the number in the household, names, current jobs and food rations clearly written on it. Our lives began to be checked and counted by this card. People who had no jobs had to move to the new economic zones, or they would get no food rations at all. Rice is very important to people because it is our country's staple food. Office workers received a ration of nine kilograms of rice and a half kilogram of meat per month and factory workers would be allowed eleven kilograms of rice and a half kilogram of meat per month.

Taking my Saigon family — seven adults and four children — as an example, we needed at least eighty kilograms of rice per month, or around two-and-a-half kilograms per day; we had also been used to having as much meat and other food as we wanted. It had been fresh and readily available in the local markets. Suddenly everything was nationalised and controlled down to the least important item. The supposed monthly food ration from the government for our seven adults was sixty-three kilograms of rice and three-and-a-half kilograms of meat per month. That was if we all had an office job. And so together with countless others we went through those early days of 'liberation' in fear, uncertainty and unemployment.

We were under constant surveillance by the district security police who were trying to force us to leave the city if we did not have a permanent job. Realising the fate of thousands of people in the new economic zones, we tried desperately to hang on where we were as long as we could. We ran around asking for work, but we were told to wait until things had settled down. In hindsight I realise we were naive to believe that we would get a job sooner or later. Unbeknown to us what was reserved for us was not a job at all, but labour in new economic zones, or being brainwashed in re-education camps.

Then came the distribution of the monthly rice rations. One morning early in the month, the loudspeaker set up at the local community hall announced, 'Rice is coming today! Rice is coming today!' Immediately people ran with a bag and the family ration card in their hands and grabbed a spot on the ground in front of the counter where rice was going to be sold at the official rate. From 9.00 a.m. until about 2.30 p.m., people sat on the dusty ground in the heat waiting for hours for their turn. Raucous bargaining and arguing were heard with the rice distributors, because people were not used to the unusual system.

Then the woman in charge announced, 'Rice has run out! All the rest come back tomorrow!'

'But we have run out of rice at home too! I can't afford to buy on the black market for my children!' a woman yelled out.

'It doesn't matter if you don't want to come back,' came the answer.

The next day we came back to collect rice and the rations were cut to forty per cent rice, and sixty per cent *do don*, rice substitutes. We were told rice had run out in the government store. The rice substitutes were some kind of flour and beans which were totally unfamiliar to us. It took people double time and double fuel to cook the beans; and we had to run around for a clue on how to make the flour into something edible. We swallowed it reluctantly for the sake of survival. I prepared about two kilograms of rice for two main meals for my family each day. It took me precisely one hour to pick out all the filth mixed in the rice ration. Not so long before, we used to feed this type of rice to our domestic animals.

I stayed awake at night. I thought of how much I had taken things for granted in our earlier life. Was it wrong to live with sufficient? Was this a kind of punishment for being capitalist? The war somehow seemed more bearable than this liberation and peace.

By now each district was watched and controlled by a northern *cong an*, security official. Each district was also divided into groups of households headed by a *to truong*, head of a group. One day we were asked to gather at our headman's home to pick a number to buy such domestic necessities as sugar, condensed milk, washing detergents and toothpaste. But there was little available. A seventeen-year-old boy stood for his family. He picked a number for just one tube of toothpaste. He was disappointed. It was not what his family needed at present. It was sugar that his mother wanted. After a few seconds, the boy said, 'I've got nothing to eat at home. Why do I need to clean my teeth?' He threw the toothpaste back on the tray.

'Mind your mouth, young man!' the headman shouted. The boy was lucky not to be reported to the local police; our *to truong* was a former soldier and an understanding man.

My father was deeply shocked when word came that a young church minister in the Mekong delta had been arrested. The local police had searched the minister's house and found in his Bible an old greeting card with greeting words written in English and a Western-style signature under-neath.

'What's this?'

'This is an old greeting card. I use it as a bookmark.'

'Nonsense! You still have some kind of connection with the Americans, don't you?'

'No, I don't. This is just something left from before. This is one of hundreds of greeting cards collected by overseas churches, and given to the children in the churches here as playthings for them. That's all. I'll throw them away if these things don't suit the new policy.' Despite the minister's explanation, it did not make sense to the new power's police. The minister was arrested.

This reminds me of a motto attributed to Ho Chi Minh: '*Bat lam hon tha lam,*' 'It's better to gaol someone by mistake than to set free someone by mistake.' Ho Chi Minh's life history records how, during his fight against the French, a couple of times Ho was caught and gaoled, suspected of being Ho Chi Minh, the leader of the anti-French move-ment; but he was released because the French at that time had no concrete evidence to prove who he really was.

After the arrest of the young minister, my father called me back to the province in order to help him clear up his small study. It was not because my father felt fear for his own life and family; but as the church representative, he hoped by doing this he would clear up any possible suspicion about the church's faith being an American religion.

It took me the whole week to clear my father's study of valuable books on education, literature and religion which he had bought, read and collected since he was a young man. In fact it would not have taken so much time if I had just simply pulled the books off the shelves and burnt them. But it was a slow struggle to throw out books deeply stained by time and see sweet family memories being turned into ash in a few moments.

I still remember how frustrated my eldest sister and I were about not being allowed to read novels. There was not a single novel on my father's bookshelves; instead there were plenty of books on education, literature, history and religion. However, later I came to love reading these so much; though on the sly we still managed to read some novels which were in fact part of our studies at high school. I still remember how much I used to enjoy browsing in that cosy room full of books and magazines and reading while the rain was falling outside. My father's study was my ideal hideaway, better than anywhere else, and each book was my best soulmate.

I asked my father to let me burn what were most likely the most dangerous books, those in English. The rest I tore into small sections, marked them carefully with my secret codes, and stored them in separate places. I still recall how nervous my mother was as she thought of the possibility of the house being searched by the police. But I said to her, 'Just say it's waste paper, Mama, if they come and check!'

Somehow I still hoped I would be able to put all the books back one day. Family photographs, greeting cards, letters which showed our friendship and relation to Americans and Australians were all destroyed. Our house became strangely bare and our hearts ached at this latest unexpected loss.

I went back to Saigon again and was startled to find the city filled with people who were demoralised by hearing others shouting: 'Down with the Imperialist US trademark. . . Down with and denounce Saigon's degenerate, depraved culture. . . Put down the southern businesses, capitalists and bourgeoisie.'

Each family and individual all of a sudden had its own dilemma to confront and to deal with every day. The new masters, instead of being reunited wonderfully with their new subjects — the stated new aim of the northern liberation forces — were for the most part arrogant, playing a confused hide-and-seek game.

Each morning people woke up to terrifying confusion about unpredictable plights they had to deal with. Every day, chaos drove people to believe at the end of the day that perhaps death was better.

A ban on American goods was not announced officially from the mouths of the people of the new power, but this propaganda was repeated all over the place: 'Down with the puppet American and their puppet products! Holding them means associating with them still, and is against the revolutionary power!'

In great fear of being accused of being against the new authorities, people dragged out countless expensive used household goods with US trademarks such as clothes, domestic electrical appliances, cutlery, even furniture from thousands of houses around Saigon, and they were sold at unbelievably low prices right in front of the house. My neighbour bitterly stated, 'It's better to get rid of them at this cheap price than to see them confiscated!'

My family in both Saigon and the province was no different. We sold almost everything—our refrigerator, television set, cutlery, furniture and a lot of the good clothes which we had been wearing. In a short time some main streets in Saigon became huge flea markets. Much later I came to the surprising realisation of who bought the US-made products from us. Who else could use them but the *Dan 30* people and our liberators from the north? Were our new masters jealous of our riches and self-sufficiency? Was the propaganda just a way to take our possessions?

Houses were checked randomly. It often happened unpredictably at night. Thousands of common useful things, old or new — in good or bad condition — such as motorbikes, bicycles, sewing machines, radio cassette recorders, cameras and so on were transferred from the owners to the hands of the local authority, because the owners were not able to present the original invoices of purchase of those items. No invoice gave the authorities the pretext of declaring them stolen goods. Customarily nobody bothered to keep an invoice for an item which had been used in the family for years. My family lost a good bicycle this way. In the same night a relative lost two bicycles.

In May 1975, the second month under the new rulers, the new administrative authority issued special orders which depressed many young people and complicated their families' situation. All students — primary to university — were ordered to return to their original schools to finish the academic year, no matter where they had been since the April turmoil. Former law students felt discouraged — those who wanted to continue their studies under the new regime first had to undergo a period of brainwashing before being allowed to transfer to other subjects.

The other instruction issued during this time was that all the registered former ARVN troops were ordered to gather at several meeting places, ready for re-education.

My eldest sister's children, Lam and Thoa, had to return to their home town Dalat in order to finish their year's studies at their original school. Tran, her husband, was preparing to say farewell.

This period provides heartbreaking memories for me. In the middle of the night I woke up to Tuyet's crying. I could not stop crying either. Lam and Thoa, children growing up in a comfortable situation with love and care, now had to face new unexpected hardships. They returned to the place where only a few months ago everything still belonged to their beloved family. They became like two lonely creatures in a desert.

Here was the road which led to their family home, but there was no home for them there any more. Here was the green hill where their family used to have a Sunday picnic with lots of fun; now the hill looked bare and cold. Here was the road bordered with tall pine trees running along the peaceful lake to the shopping area. They passed the small gift shop which used to be run by their mother and a relative; now the shop was empty. Dalat is an elegant town located on the lavish, green highlands of central Vietnam where the average temperature of seventeen degrees Celsius had made it a tiny European haven amidst the tropical scenery. It is named by the Vietnamese the *Xu Suong Mu*, 'Land of Mist'. It is beautiful. But its beauty was clouded in loneliness.

Lam and Thoa had to stay for two months in Dalat in the temporary care of a relative. They went back to their original school to finish their school year in order to be permitted to enter a public school in Saigon. When they returned to Saigon, their military father had gone to pay the price of being a soldier and a capitalist.

One evening the *cong an*, district security police, came to warn us to get rid of everything foreign in our house before the 'Down with the depraved culture' campaign took place in our district. Everybody in my family was sure there was nothing left to be worried about. But it was not so. There was one 'depraved cultural thing' which I had treasured and intended to keep for myself as long as I could. It was all the letters which Bruce had written to me over the years.

That night seemed too short for me to think whether or not I should get rid of them for the sake of my family's security. I thought of many different ways to hide them, but nothing sounded really safe. At one moment I thought how silly I was in keeping those things of the past, but at the next moment I saw them as cherished memories. However, knowing that I had been registered as one of the imperialist American local employees, I knew I was in danger. A beautiful part of my self disappeared as the vivid blue-inked handwriting rapidly vanished in the silent flames.

In late September 1975, the exchange of old Saigon's 'puppet dong' to the new dong of the Bank of Vietnam officially took place in the south. The official exchange was 500 old dong to one new dong. Each individual's money had to be registered as well as deposited in the government bank, the Bank of Vietnam. A maximum of 100 000 of the old dong could be exchanged for 200 new dong per adult. All the excess monies had to be entrusted to the bank. Any future plans of withdrawal had to be approved by the local district police who would decide whether or not 'your reason to spend the money is adequate and acceptable'.

Many people in the south — especially the Chinese Vietnamese —had many times the 100 000 dong limit (equivalent to about US $200 in 1975) which the new authority would allow people to exchange for the new currency. What were we supposed to do with all the rest of the money? The people of Saigon did not want to entrust their wealth to the new power, especially under the new system of withdrawal. They believed they would never get their money back. What would happen if people hid the money at home and did not register it? Surely the money would be worthless as it was the old unusable currency.

The nature of this new monetary policy and the too short notice given for the currency exchange knocked most southern people down like a sudden epidemic, brutally sweeping over the entire land. Within a short time there seemed no-one left with any confidence in the 'peace' provided by the liberating power.

On the last day of the currency exchange due date, two close friends suddenly visited our family. They were from a well-known business family who owned one of the few high-class restaurants in Dalat, the Mekong Restaurant. One of them showed us a handful of money and said to my sister Tuyet: 'We think it's better to share this money with your family and some other close friends who have lost their homes and money in Dalat than to entrust it to the bank. We actually have much more than they allow us to have.' We had been close friends with this family over many years. They were hardworking people and had built up their business from nothing.

On that last day, many people in the same situation silently rushed around the city to scatter their fortune among their relatives, friends and even neighbours who could use it to make up the limit which could be exchanged.

I remember how nervous and confused my mother and other neighbours were when they held the one new dong in their hands. 'Will this be worth 500 old dong?' People became terrified! At first simple minds thought if the price of an item which they bought yesterday was 500 dong, today they would pay only one new dong for the same thing.

But it was not as simple as that. Five hundred dong used to be sufficient for an average family's needs of fresh food, meat and rice for a day; now one new dong was just enough to buy a daily rice ration for an average family, nothing else.

Some people had a humorous comment that the value of the Vietnamese new currency sounded as strong as US dollars. Not so long before the fall of Saigon, one US dollar was equivalent to 500 dong in the south. The difference between then and now was that, whereas a monthly low income for a southerner was 20 000 dong (equivalent to forty US dollars), under the new administration an office worker received twenty dong monthly (equivalent to four US dollars), a thousand per cent decrease. More significantly, the present inflation rate was more than twice the decrease in the value of the dong. In reality, the Vietnamese new 'dollar' was as light as ash.

People were educated to hate the American, the invader of the nation. Yet the northerners started to enjoy the leftovers from the imperialists. When they wanted to buy something of their own, they definitely looked for the US trademark on the goods. But whenever their ego was hurt by lack of knowledge of how to adjust to daily life in Saigon, they would furiously claim, 'That's a trick left by *thang My*, the rascal Americans!'

It was widely known that these northern people were skilled people sent to the south to help establish the new land. They occupied all the properties, buildings, villas, residences and houses around Saigon which were left behind by wealthy owners who had fled the city in April. Some larger residences were partly occupied even though the actual family was still living there. Later, the cadres' families from Hanoi came south to join them.

Living in those modern residences was a crisis for the northerners rather than a victorious pleasure in the early days. They were known to have panicked when the toilet was blocked because the bowl was used to wash clothes; when it was flushed, their clothes would disappear down the hole.

A man who ran a photo shop admitted that he had actually made quite a bit of easy money over the previous few months. Most of his customers were from the north. Whether they were cadres or civilians, they loved to have one or two colour photographs taken with some special thing they had dreamed of buying in Saigon.

The most popular photograph was one with their smiling face and their left arm prominent, showing a waterproof watch. That was what fascinated them. That was what they were after when they came to a Saigon shop. That was what they would proudly show to their family and friends when they returned to Hanoi. 'Do you have *dong ho co ao mua*, a watch with a raincoat?'

One day I asked a friend's relative, a cadre or government official, 'Why do you educate us to hate the Americans, but still want to use their things?' His answer was very direct. 'We hate the Americans, but we like things made by them. Their products are excellent.'

A special visit by a northern cadre to Saigon during the early days of their liberation of the south would conclude by his buying an electric fan to take home. The whole family and friends would crowd into the house to enjoy the 'electric breeze' instead of the 'hand-made breeze' from paper fans.

Contact between the Saigon people and the northerners was unavoidable. I came to know a Hanoi young woman who had been in Saigon for a short time. Her husband was a trained technician and she was a government officer. She seemed an honest person who could express exactly what was in her mind, though not publicly.

She told me, 'Soon after the liberation, I told my husband that at any cost we must be transferred to the south. We were so lucky to be assigned to the new jobs. Then we sold our house and I told my husband I would keep the money to buy rice, the one thing I dreamt of for my four children. All their lives they have rarely had rice, only *do don*, rice substitutes.' Dried manioc was the common staple food northerners ate all year round. For a normal meal, it was sprinkled with hot chilli salt.

She admitted that the sale of her family house in Hanoi was only worth 100 kilograms of rice in Saigon. Although, in those early months after the takeover, Saigon was not yet under total control economically, she hid the rice under her bed in the bedroom for fear of being discovered and reported to the local police as being influenced by the capitalists.

Her children loved Saigon's instant noodle. However, she said, the children would cheer up if she said, 'We'll eat rice today!' And her voice softened: 'The propaganda made the Hanoi people believe that the southerners were hungry and ragged under capitalism. We were told Hanoi's people must try to tighten their belts in order to liberate the south.'

At first I was very cautious of being spied upon by this woman, but later I came to appreciate her integrity which I had thought impossible under the new regime. Another time she told me, 'My relative is one of the key people of the "Down with the Saigon depraved culture" campaign as a result of which a lot of Saigon music tapes have been confiscated. It's beautiful music and delightful singing! I've never heard anything as nice before.'

'How do you know what it's like?' I asked.

'Instead of destroying the tapes, my relative secretly brought them home. We hid in the room and listened to them all.'

'My family had to throw all ours out!' I said.

'It's a pity,' the woman said. 'If I'd known you before, I would have kept them for you.' How similar to us these people were, I thought. They want and like the same things that we do. Later the northerners called Saigon's former music *nhac vang*, the golden music. In private, knowing this music was considered sophisticated.

I felt the defeat of the south had liberated the north from insane hardship and useless ideology.

Word came from my mother in the province that she had had to let all my 'stored waste paper' go because it was not safe to keep it any more. It was sold by weight, per kilogram.

At a Saigon bus station one day my sister Tram saw a small boy selling snacks. He wrapped the food in the pages torn from Bibles.

10

Re-education:
late 1970s

THE PROMISED TEN-DAY PERIOD of brainwashing former
ARVN officers was over. But families saw no sign of their
loved ones returning home. None of the families knew
where the re-education centres were.

Six months had passed since the change of regime. Life
could be likened to being dragged down an endless slope.
Most of the men had suddenly vanished from the women's
and children's lives, and been taken to mysterious destina-
tions. The women were left to fight for their survival while
being mistreated and rejected by the new power.

How to get a permanent job so that their families would
not be forced to go to the new ecomonic zones? How to keep
their children in schools, but away from the new atheist
doctrine? Party, not family, was made the children's first
priority. Everything came from hard labour, not from prayers.

Religion was supposed to be a kind of drug which only
lulled people into disabling laziness. How to keep the
family property and avoid its being confiscated for no good
reason? How to hide one's background from the persecution that would result from being linked with the former
regime or with the Americans? These were some of thousands of complications of the new way of life.

The struggle to combat these hardships left the women no time to think of where their spouse was. Until one day Tuyet — my eldest sister — was quietly approached by a group of women whose husbands were in the same situation as hers.

'It's not right not to know where they are. We must get together and *xuong duong*, demonstrate, to question the authorities about where all our men are and find out how much longer before they are allowed to come home.'

Early one morning a crowd of women gathered in front of the Saigon Catholic cathedral situated in an area close to the centre of the city. All were very emotional and self-conscious.

'What are you doing here, women?' the police shouted.

'We need to know where our husbands are — and when they are returning home,' the women answered. 'Could we see the authority in charge, please?'

'None of your business!' the police replied. 'Who's put pressure on you to ask these questions?'

The women did not yet realise that they were surrounded by a crowd of angry police.

'But the government said it would be only for ten days. It's two months now,' a woman shouted.

'Who told you it would be ten days? It depends on how good your men are in their repentance to the liberators and the Party before they can be returned home. Now shut up and go home!' the police said firmly.

Then another woman broke from the crowd of women and dashed up to the police with an old newspaper in her hand, the *Saigon Giai Phong*, the 'Saigon Liberation'. She pointed to the newspaper and cried out nervously, 'It's from the mouth of the government! It's printed in here! It says ten days!'

'It's from the paper, not from the police!' came back the

false answer from the police. 'Go away or you yourselves will be put in gaol. Which do you prefer, women?' Then the police got on their bicycles and pedalled off.

'Liar! Liar! It's you who need to be re-educated, not our men!' the woman screamed. Finally all dispersed bitterly, disappointed that they were leaving the silent cathedral behind as the only witness of the real truth.

That same morning the 'friendly local police' — friendliness is claimed as the basis on which the local police could come into people's houses at any time for a quiet search or to provide criticism — called on my family and asked me if my eldest sister had gone to the demonstration.

'I'm afraid I don't know,' I replied. 'She left home early as usual for a day of trading.'

'How silly those women are!' He smiled faintly. 'No such thing is to be tolerated under the communist government. They've got to learn to be quiet, otherwise they will be re-educated and their family food rations will be cut off.'

My memory was still as fresh as if it had been just the previous day when Tran, my eldest sister's husband, had left our home for the re-education camp. Though extremely concerned and sad for his family's uncertain situation, Tran's willingness to become a normal citizen under the new regime helped him control his emotions when he said goodbye to us all.

Though a different doctrine was surely operating, Tran counted on the justice espoused by the new regime. He thought things might not be as bad as the Thieu government had claimed. Tran in fact had been a victim of the injustice under the former government when corruption was widely evident, especially throughout military circles. Tran, a trained engineer and captain in the army, had received an honest upbringing, and was determined to live an honest life as a loyal subject of his country. Yet when he refused to take part in the corrupt practices of his direct boss — a military major — he was victimised and the target of vengeful acts.

I remember once Tran was requested to produce a detailed plan for a large construction. His boss instructed him to make the price three times the actual cost. This extra would be split secretly between the boss, the private contractor who would sign the building contract, and Tran himself.

Tran's opposition in this matter at first brought the contractor — under the major's advice — to the back door of his home believing that his opposition was actually a bargaining tactic to increase his share. The contractor handed a large amount of money to Tran's small children as a New Year gift.

When the money was rejected, Tran's military boss knew that the only way to gild his road to wealth was to dump Tran for someone else who would collaborate in the scheme. Tran was sent to a remote military post without his family and nothing to do. Finally, his wife was forced to plead for his rescue through a powerful man who was a close friend of Tran's family.

Tran now believed he would return home after only ten days of being re-educated, just as he and the thousands of other former military officers had been told by the new masters. He even refused to take things which seemed basic needs for a long trip. One of my brothers gave Tran a ride on his bicycle to the nearby public primary school, one of the gathering points of the future prisoners. There they said a simple goodbye, for he was convinced they would see each other again soon.

Tran took with him a large plastic carrying bag in which were two sets of worn-out clothes, a bath towel, some underclothes, a toothbrush and toothpaste — very limited equipment even for ten days. Yet these few things turned out to be the most valued possessions on Tran's unwanted journey.

Time became meaningless. One day Tran realised that he was at least 2 000 kilometres away from his home and family. He and other former ARVN officers, blindfolded and handcuffed, had been transported day and night from place to place in covered trucks and then on trains to the most remote areas near the Chinese border.

There he began a life of peace — a dead peace provided by his liberators. Tran, the prisoner without a court case or a personal verdict, had to turn in to himself for comfort. 'I am still confident of this,' Tran whispered to himself in tears. 'Oh Lord! I would have despaired unless I had believed that I would see the goodness of the Lord in the land of the living.'

However, my brother-in-law admitted that the 2 555 days of forced collective labour on the edge of life and death, the costly toll of being brainwashed to emptiness, the loneliness and the isolation almost caused him to give up hope. This man who had always resisted corruption in the past had to pray hard many times not to steal another prisoner's survival rations. His stomach was constantly left empty as punishment for being sick and frail most of the time and for not being able to fulfil all that was required of him.

One day during a move to another labour area, a young former ARVN captain, a fellow exile, took a risk in tempting a young *bo doi*, northern soldier, into exchanging a tin of out-of-date condensed milk for his old military jacket. That night under the ragged leaking roof of a tent in the silent darkness, the young man whispered jokingly to Tran: 'Dear comrade! Do you believe you still receive benefit from the *My Nguy*, the Americans and their puppet army? Get up and have a bit of milk I bought for you.'

The elderly Buddhist monk who lived in a temple on the outskirts of Saigon could not understand what was actually inside the heavy trucks, thickly covered by dark green plastic sheets, as they moved along the road in the middle of the night. But his spiritual sensitivity woke him earlier than normal the following morning for a special silent prayer. Then he went for a walk. The tracks of those mysterious trucks were still seen deep in the earthen road. He noticed something apparently insignificant, a small bit of paper, crumpled into a ball on the edge of the grass. He quickly picked it up and went back to his temple. He opened it and read, *Ra Bac — bien gioi Tau,* 'Going north — Chinese border.'

From that day the news of where the former ARVN men were going was passed on to whoever visited his temple. My eldest sister and her three friends heard of this and went to see the monk secretly.

After a long rugged journey on the cattle trucks that made up the train from Saigon to Hanoi, then by antique buses, my sister and her friends finally sat down under a tiny thatched shelter in an unknown place and filled in the application forms for the permit to see their husbands in the re-education camps.

Across the top of the gate in front of a range of thatched huts, Ho Chi Minh's motto was painted in red on a large tin sheet. It was like a hard bullet penetrating into the human heart: *Khong co gi quy hon doc lap, tu do va hanh phuc,* 'Nothing is more precious than independence, freedom and happiness.' To the women, these very qualities had been destroyed. They were like innocent high-flying doves unable to help themselves from being shot down by a violent gunman.

In the hazy distance in the fading light that afternoon, my sister and her friends saw a quiet crowd draw closer to the area where they were. They felt anxious. It was more than a year since their unexpected separation. It seemed ages since their families' happiness had been traumatically locked behind the gate with the painted words of freedom and happiness. But the special visit could not happen until the next day.

'*Having* nothing is *far* more precious than *this* independence, freedom and happiness.' Those little words added to Ho Chi Minh's motto were not just a childish joke; they emphasised the bitter, contradictory experiences southern people had gone through since the communist takeover.

The 'freedom' meant thousands of innocent people were imprisoned. The 'unification' between north and south meant a division of hatred. The 're-education' was a cruel expression of revenge rather than understanding, torture rather than healing.

The national logo *Xa Hoi Chu Nghia* or *XHCN*, 'Socialist Republic', was like a holy title and always had to be stated on any legal papers above the slogan 'Independence, Freedom and Happiness'. The word game people played with this was to use the actual first letter of each word of the title — *XHCN* — then repeat it twice to make up a phrase which expressed their agony about the truth: for example, *Xep hang con nguoi, xuong hang cho ngua* translates literally 'Categorising human beings down to the level of dogs and horses'. This play on words expressed the gap between government slogan and reality.

I have a clear picture in my mind of the crowd as I gathered with them at the large community hall at least four nights a week to be 'educated' about the new regime's policies. The evenings were humid and stuffy and the meeting place had a dirty, dusty cement floor. We sat on the floor absolutely exhausted after a hard day's work, often 'forced volunteer' day labour for us jobless people. We longed for sleep rather than anything else.

'Ho Chi Minh muon nam!', 'Long live! Long live!' came the faint response from the crowd with hands raised and lowered, tired and aching. One evening a baby at its mother's breast suddenly cried out. The mother was harshly criticised by the leader that she had tried to create a reason to leave the meeting too soon.

The forced education sessions lasted about two hours each evening, during which the same things were repeated over and over: 'The imperialist American, the CIA, still puts people back here to work for them, twisting the words of the government's slogans to undermine the value of this regime.' Or, '"Watch and Report" is the responsibility of all and is a good contribution to the peace of this country.' Or, 'Self-consciousness and self-criticism in public is a must in order to purify ourselves to be suitable for this communist heaven' — 'heaven' was the word they actually used.

A new regulation was announced. A travel permit had to be obtained at the local police office — giving reason, length of time and destination — before going on a trip beyond one's own town. At the destination, people had to register their names with the local police. Otherwise, after a random check at night, people would be regarded as criminals, no matter if it was only a normal visit of family members to their family home.

By this time almost everything was controlled by the new government. Private businesses, both big and small, were not allowed to operate. The basic materials for daily living, such as rice, meat, sugar, coffee beans, medicines and petrol, became scarce. These goods were reserved for the cadres and government workers and were sold only at government shops.

Public hospitals were reserved for high government cadres and their families only. The local dispensaries were available for average people for all sorts of sickness. The only medicine people were likely to receive for most illness was *Xuyen tam lien*, a tablet of mixed Oriental herbs.

Throughout the country electricity was cut off every second day. People were arrested if seen carrying any forbidden goods. Paradoxically, black markets appeared with all these things, but at unbelievably high prices, so high that most people could not afford to buy them. Who could afford them? people wondered.

It took a great effort to adjust to the new regime, but some of our family members were able to do so sufficiently to get a simple job. My sister Tuyet was an assembly worker with a *to hop*, a small co-op team under government surveillance, but run by an old friend who had tried to adapt to the new life, and help friends who were not able to help themselves in this difficult situation. He knew how to make soy sauce out of soya beans. His small work team consisted of people like my sister and other wives and family workers of former ARVN men who could never hope to be employed by the government.

Some members of my family were thought to have an acceptable record by the new authority, because in the former regime they were only privates in the army, or students. They were thought not too dangerous. They were given clerical jobs. Their attitudes towards the new atheist philosophy, however, were tested. They were watched. Their strong traditional background would not lead them to great success in a society where success depended on becoming a member of the Party. The longer a person had been in the Party, the better. Their pride was their years of membership. Success only came for them in this life. Life after death was something not to be concerned about.

An acquaintance gave me some advice. As I spoke English, I should try to get a job at, say, the Office of Tourism, where he thought people were sure to welcome my contribution. I went to some offices and put my application forms in; but I was never asked to see them for a job.

At the same time, the local security policeman regularly visited me at home with my past work record in his hands. He repeated the same questions over and over about my old job. This confused me greatly. 'It depends on your good, honest attitude which will help to annul your past, and straighten out your future.' This was a communist formula to explain everything, that explained nothing. I applied for several other jobs, but was refused each time. I sensed discriminatory treatment because of my working with foreigners in the past; but I believed my honesty would eventually help and my life would become normal under the new regime.

A girlfriend of mine who had been a long-term staff member of a private foreign firm hid her work identity for fear of being sent to a re-education camp. She also hoped that it would help her to be treated as a normal citizen. She advised me to do the same. The fear of being convicted of a 'double crime' — a loyalist of the imperialists and a liar to the liberators — was greater than anything else. I had already reported myself to the security police as to who I was in the past.

As I did not have a proper job, I had to lean on the small earnings of my brothers and sisters. In fact with the overall economic collapse, most people were not able to stand on their own two feet.

The average wage of an office worker was twenty dong per month, but the price of petrol in the market was five hundred dong per litre, and two to three dong per tablet for common headaches, only available from a secret retailer. During this time private doctors still managed to practice unnoticed by the authorities, but refused to assist patients — though seriously ill — if their own families required any of the scarce medicines. Western medicines which had been used throughout the south for generations completely disappeared on the public markets; but on the black markets they were gold.

Trade became a stopgap way of making a living for most people. This involved buying goods or food from one place and selling them at another place for a profit. If they were forbidden goods supplied on the black market, traders would make considerable profits — an extremely risky way to make money.

Just like many others, I bought and sold different sorts of things to make a living. But my trade involved only small things and not forbidden goods; therefore the profit was so tiny that I was not able to make ends meet.

However, the trade — small or big — was like another 'Hide-and-seek' game between people and the communist police. If the traders were caught, the capital invested in their goods would be confiscated by the police. Once, my sister and I were on the way from the province to the city. A woman got on the bus with her heavy luggage — three big shopping baskets — and sat next to us. Looking at her and her luggage, we knew instantly that it was illegal trade. With her left foot, she gradually pushed her two baskets underneath our seats.

'Dear me,' Tram whispered to me, 'this woman's going to give us a problem! She's going to ignore her illegal baskets if there is a check from the police. Or the two baskets will be considered ours because they are under our seats.'

'What will we do?' I asked Tram. We pretended to talk loudly to each other that we had forgotten to buy something else. We got off the bus; then we came back again and sat in the back of the bus to avoid this woman. Later things happened exactly as we feared. The police caught her and the two women who filled our previous seats.

In time, there were more small traders than buyers and the trade collapsed.

Personal economic crises were increasing due to the national controls on all economic activity. Even loving and supportive families like mine somehow could not avoid emotional crises as a result of the depressed economy. Each member suffered different losses and regrets. Bitterness and anger would sometimes erupt, causing frightful misunderstandings between one another.

One day, feeling so down and depressed I could not help it, I complained about how I could not live in this awful situation much longer. I sensed my complaint had a really bad effect on Ly, my nineteen-year-old brother. He quietly left the room. Perhaps he needed to vent his frustration over my unpleasant complaint. I regretted what I had said after he had gone. He is a loving brother and I have loved him dearly.

Nobody minded doing any odd job to make some extra income in order to survive. It was no surprise if a professor became a bicycle repairer working on the street or an engineer turned to pedicab driving. With a motorbike available and spare time after working hours, some could make several such trips around Saigon. A motorbike became a treasure for someone who still owned one.

My brother left home riding his motorbike. It was one of the few valuable things we were determined to keep — not to sell it foolishly like many others. The motorbike was our family's financial security. Two hours later, the familiar sound of his motorbike was heard stopping at the front door. From inside the house I saw my brother turn his motorbike to park on the veranda. Blood was running down his arms, soaking his dark-coloured shirt.

'Oh God! What's happening? Sisters! Quick!' I called out, terrified.

I held my brother in my arms just as he was about to collapse. His face was pale and his voice feeble. A large wound ran down the back of his head. Not bothering to learn what had caused this, we immediately rushed him to hospital. It was a hospital where we happened to know a doctor. The help from him was tremendous.

Ly was in a coma. The doctor was concerned that his brain might have been damaged. He did everything he could for him, but warned us that if by midnight my brother had not woken up normally and shown some sign of recovery, then his brain would have lost its chance of coming back to normal. The doctor explained that my brother had been hit by an iron bar from behind. There was no doubt about what had happened. Someone had tried to attack him so that they could steal his motorbike. Somehow Ly, though seriously wounded, still managed to get back home on his motorbike.

That night I sat next to my brother on the edge of his bed, waiting for him to wake up. Tears of love were flowing from the bottom of my broken heart. How could this kind of brutality be happening to our family? We were not dangerous people; rather, we wished to live in kindness and justice. Before 1975, we had never faced this kind of fury. The wicked had their own ways and we had ours.

'Dear God, please wake him up!' I prayed from my heart and soul. 'Please, God! Otherwise I will live in sorrow and regret for the rest of my life. Because it was I who caused the accident!'

By midnight Ly woke up. His mind was clear and accurate. Ly told us he had fought against the man who attacked him, using his bare hands and a silent prayer.

A few weeks later, after visiting our parents in the province, my sister and I went back to Saigon. On the crowded bus, we saw a seven-year-old boy being pushed by his mother to carry a heavy straw bag onto the bus. The bag in fact was full of fresh meat — a prohibited item of commerce — hidden under various objects. My sister and I actually knew these people very well; they had been living in the same town as my parents. The little boy used to be one of the children in the preschool which was formerly sponsored by foreign aid donations.

The young woman told us frankly that she was trying to make enough to live by doing this trade, taking things to the black market in Saigon. She used her son to carry the goods as if he was the owner of the goods. Whenever her secret trade was revealed, her small son would run away from the police easily. If this happened, her goods would be seized by the police, but she herself would not be caught, and the secret trade would be continued the next day.

This little boy in fact was of mixed Vietnamese and American blood. Whatever the background, I sensed deeply the pain of being abandoned when I looked at his innocent face. With his blond hair, brown eyes and fair complexion, this boy bore all the marks of Western sophistication. Yet here he was, an unwanted creature lost in poverty and hardship. He was one of the modern *Les Miserables*.

We were shocked to hear that the latest provincial police order required all my father's sermons to be censored before being preached in churches. But my father — though he was not unaware of increased difficulties under this new administration — thought that this would be a wonderful opportunity for the communists to hear of God's words. My father prayed to this effect.

He was devastated to see some preachers turn their backs on their flock. Some were fearful of repercussions if they spoke against the atheistic doctrine. Some were tempted by some kind of favour from the communists which would make their life easier. One such person was a minister who wished to bring in some 'fresh air from the revolution'. When his idea was not supported, he became a stumbling-block to the church. Unlike many other churches which witnessed a magnificent increase in faith, my parents sadly experienced the opposite.

Once my father was arrested by the communists. He was pressed to make some major changes in church structure. Pastors should be in the forced labour teams and should earn their own living. Money offerings were not allowed in the church. Youth, teenagers' and children's activities organised by the churches were forbidden. It did not matter how much pressure they tried to put on my father, he did not yield. Everywhere the church activities were restricted. Some church properties came under police surveillance, or were partly used by the local authorities as public meeting places and for other similar purposes.

My parents' home, once a cosy retreat, had turned into a place of sadness, fear and heartbreak.

One morning, Thy, one of my brothers who was in his teens, went out with his best school friend for a cup of coffee at the local coffee shop. Soon after, my parents were terrified to hear from his friend that my brother had been arrested by the local police for no apparent reason. My father went to see the local police, but they refused to tell him the reason. *'Ly do cho biet sau'*, 'The reason is to be given later,' they said. This is the phrase people normally hear from the police for something they refuse to explain.

Eight weeks later, even though my father had not yet found out where my brother was detained, Thy was released unexpectedly. We felt such relief and were grateful for the police making the right judgment. However, former prisoners had to report themselves monthly at the local security police station until their security records were considered completely clear. This period could be three months, six months or one year. My brother was given one year's probation though he was only an eight-week prisoner.

After being released from gaol, Thy did not say much about why he had been arrested. My parents thought that the incident that led to his arrest was related to some characteristic teenage behaviour. It was the first bad experience for him under the new regime. So we tried to be sensitive to him, and did not ask what the reason was. Thy was not accepted back in school after his release from gaol.

Eight months later, one morning Thy again went to the police office for his monthly report. But this time he did not come back home as usual. Thy's friend was waiting for him to come out of the police station to have a cup of coffee with him at a nearby shop. A police truck suddenly drove past. From it he heard my brother shout, 'Take my bicycle back home, will you?' The message was not clear, but succeeded in getting the attention of his friend in the coffee shop. His friend was sensitive enough to know Thy was arrested again.

The next day, my father went to see the police. 'I'd like to know the reason,' my father said.

'Don't worry, Uncle!' The policeman seemed very

pleasant. 'He should be fine when he comes back.'

'I believe what you've said. But can't I know the reason why he's been arrested?' my father insisted.

'But he has not been arrested!' the policeman said. 'He'll be learning the value of labour, that's all. Everybody's got to know about labour anyway.'

'How long before he will be allowed to come home?' my father asked.

'It depends on how good he is,' the policeman answered.

'Can I have a permit to visit my son?' my father asked.

'We'll let you know later,' the policeman answered coolly. Three months later, my family finally heard where Thy had been detained.

The police did not inform families where prisoners were. Forced labour camps were not located at fixed places and were often in remote areas; and the prisoner's family had to find it for themselves. But once everything was found out, it was the family's responsibility to supply the prisoner with dried food for his survival.

Thy was held as a prisoner for more than two years. When he came out, he told us the real story behind it.

In high school, Thy and some other friends were very fond of one of their teachers. In their leisure time after school they used to visit this teacher at his home. He often talked with them about the communist resistance groups as if they were part of his dream. Thy did not know that his teacher was in fact the leader of one small resistance group at work around that area. Thy was arrested because he was seen in the teacher's home the night before. The teacher was also arrested at the same time, but Thy did not know.

A complicating issue for my brother was that the police knew he knew nothing about the resistance. But they wanted an excuse to put pressure on him in another important matter — to spy on the local church and on our father! The probationary release was given only for him to make a monthly report on this 'job' to the secret police. My brother would not do such a thing to the church or our father; but his false promise to the police was the only way he could be released from gaol. He had been threatened by the police with repercussions if he said anything about this to either my parents or anybody else.

The second arrest was because after eight months of expecting a lot of information from my brother, his report still read, 'Nothing has been seen.' He was therefore sent to the labour camp for not being cooperative with the authorities.

During this time rumour spread around the city that there would soon be a coup directed by the *Nguy*, the former ARVN groups hiding in the jungles, to overthrow the new government and restore the Republic of Vietnam.

In the early days of the takeover, many people did hope for a miracle that would result in a change to what they called *Mot cuoc doi doi*, 'Coming back to the former life.'

As people say, in the darkest night the stars shine the brightest — there are always comforts which emerge to ease our suffering.

This proved to be true when my family and I unexpectedly met a woman who came from the north and who had a remarkable story. She was born in Saigon, but was believed to have been lost during the French period. Her story begins with the sudden death of her young mother. As a little girl she migrated with her father and his new wife to Vientiane, Laos. Poverty and hardship in the strange land gradually took the lives of her father and stepmother, leaving her in the hands of her step-grandmother.

In 1954, northern Vietnam was transferred from the French to Ho Chi Minh, in accordance with the Geneva Accords. The northern authorities ordered all Vietnamese expatriates to return home to the north, because peace was now claimed to have been achieved in that part of the country. And so the lonely grandmother, who was originally from the north, left the foreign country where she had buried all her loved ones and went back to her homeland with her step-grandchild. But life there produced further hardship for the elderly woman, even in her own land, so she soon passed away. Her step-grandchild had now become a young woman. She had grown up being completely out of touch with her natural mother's family, except for a vague memory that her mother was from south Vietnam. She dreamed of marrying a man from the south who had gone north in 1954, hoping one day she would be able to go back to the south with him and find her natural mother's family. She was actually an ordinary woman with little education; but everything happened for her just as if she were her own fortune-teller.

She met him. He was a Viet minh soldier from the south who was forced to regroup to the north after the battle of Dien Bien Phu. The ex-Viet minh soldier had lived out his youth being extremely exploited by the northern government. He was now a mature, strong-willed man.

During 1959 and 1960, the communist guerilla units were formed, and moved south to fight against the 'American imperialists and their puppet army'. All the southern ex-Viet minh in the north were forced to become Viet Cong guerillas, the only way for them to return to the south. He refused to go south. He predicted that the hard labour and training to fight along the mysterious Ho Chi

Minh trail would kill him before he actually saw the land of his birth. Even the promised food ration for a guerilla, about five times more than the standard ration for a northern civilian, did not persuade him. Instead, though missing his home, he fought to stay in Hanoi and to have an education, a career and proper shelter. Then he met the woman, the lost child of the south, and together their dreams came true when they migrated to the south.

Had this former Viet minh not fought against going down the deadly Ho Chi Minh trail, he might well have died and would not have had the chance to see his motherland again. Had he not fought against poverty and hardship to get an education and a career, he would now have been illiterate. Had he not fought against loneliness and misery until he found a southern wife, he would not have had a good reason to return to the south after the peace had come. So all his life was fighting.

Yet the ex-fighter actually had a kind heart. Though he had been shut behind the iron curtain, he tried to build a bridge of understanding. Under the bridge he was trying to build, he kept seeing the ceaseless flowing waters wash away the good he sought to do.

'Well, my dear son! How can I say goodbye to you?' this cadre said emotionally to his young relative whose father was a former ARVN soldier and who was trying to escape. 'It means I will never see you again.' He paused for a moment. 'Anyway, be clever this time and get away from this gaol.'

His relative did escape and, one day, this cadre received a short letter from overseas. He read it with a little confused sadness. 'Dear brother Phong, if the Vietnamese communists had all been like you, I would not have chosen the life of a exile.'

11

The dangerous road to freedom: 1979 – 1981

'THE LORD IS MY SHEPHERD, I shall not be in want. He makes me lie down in green pastures. . .'

The middle-aged pastor put his Bible down on the pulpit, took off his glasses with one hand, and with the other leant against the edge of the wooden stand. He raised his eyes, looking over the people sitting in the church, as if he would like to capture the real thoughts in people's minds at that moment.

Suddenly he stood up straight and cried out, 'What does "the green pastures" mean to you? Please tell me.'

We were all quiet. This chapter of the Bible was familiar to all of us. We knew it by heart. But what was the pastor's teaching this time? He seemed serious, almost bitter.

'Does it mean where there are a lot of dollars?'

Sitting next to me, Mrs Huong — a member of the church committee — suddenly touched me lightly on my arm. 'Dear me, he knows everything!' she murmured.

'What do you mean, "he knows everything"?' I whispered.

'What else would you think if it's not about us planning to leave sooner or later?' Again Mrs Huong's voice was merely a murmur.

Like Mrs Huong, I felt nervous and confused. I did not know whether or not the pastor really knew about our personal plans; but there was no doubt that many southerners had begun working on their heartbreaking secret plan, the escape to life.

The atmosphere and people's attitude were like they had been in that unforgettable April of 1975. In secret, hopes and wishes of leaving Vietnam were interlaced with confusion and stress. It was a poignant decision which would affect all things of life, a lifetime bargain with oneself, for better or for worse, for life or death. My sisters and I were no different from many of these people.

The rest of the sermon on that Sunday morning was lost as I pondered the words: 'Where are the green pastures?' This tortured my heart.

Four years had now passed since the communist takeover, two years since my first failed escape attempt in the jungle in 1977. On that occasion, together with the other escapees and some members of our family, we were arrested and imprisoned.

Why did we try to escape the first time? How was this idea implanted in our minds? I have never forgotten that it all began with my eldest sister. One day she returned home from work in a state of hidden excitement. For the first time a close friend had conveyed to her the idea of leaving. Her friend was thrilled to be asked by a Chinese businessman to become secretly involved with him in organising the escape from Vietnam. Known as a trusted person in his community, her friend would be the Chinese businessman's secret liaison. He would convince the wealthy people — especially the Chinese — who wished to join the escape to life.

The enormous amount of money involved was not the

only problem; leaving was a dangerous, criminal act which would involve many risks. However, our friend Louis — a former primary schoolteacher — explained that he had accepted the difficult job for the sake of a better life for himself and his family. If he succeeded, he could go free-of-charge.

This idea was amazing, far beyond our thoughts and expectations. We had thought up to this time that only the rich could afford to escape. But in practice, how would the escape be organised? How could such a criminal task be carried out without the communist police and spies learning about it? It sounded absolutely impossible to people like us who had been securely locked behind the iron curtain.

However, my sisters and I were attracted by our friend's idea. We had so little money, almost nothing compared to others, yet we expected a miracle.

I was in quite a state. I was an unwanted person. I was in constant fear that sooner or later I would be sent to prison to be re-educated. I had not seen any hope of being considered a normal person in this new society. From a hard-working person who was able to handle life generally, I suddenly became a hungry loafer. It was a humiliating punishment. Death was emerging from life.

My eldest sister, though with different concerns, was in no better a situation. There was no hope for her and her family now. She would be persecuted in one way or another. She had no right to live close to her husband. Her children's future — as the children of an ex-military officer and a capitalist — was shattered by their tarnished reputation, no matter how bright or capable they were. In fact, a motto promoted by the Vietnamese communists was *Trong cay muoi nam, trong nguoi mot tram nam*, 'It takes ten years to grow a tree, but a hundred years to grow a person.' The

communist did not care if the 'half-and-half' present generation disappeared. The authorities would start a new
generation which could be totally manipulated by a purely
atheistic doctrine.

Through our friend's considerable effort as liaison, and
our small contribution of money as part of his own family,
four members of our family, including myself, were secretly
added to the list. Not knowing what challenges would lie
ahead, we gave ourselves to this most dangerous adventure.

Nevertheless this escape turned out to be a deception.
Neither our friend nor we knew the true situation. We
were like babes in arms, caught up in something we did
not understand.

The new authority, following its strategy of 'Down with
the Chinese businesses', had in effect expelled the wealthy
Chinese from Vietnam. They forced them to use their
fortune in pure gold to buy their way out of Vietnam. The
rich Chinese, after paying the officials off, would organise
to leave Vietnam with the connivance of the authority, a
procedure called *Di ban chinh thuc,* half-legal leaving. They
were guided by the local communist marines through
Vietnam's territorial waters where the Chinese boats would
become refugees' boats.

This method provided a possible passage to freedom for
Vietnamese suffering politically. They begged to be allowed to join the Chinese. They used Chinese false names
and paid in gold.

However, our liaison contact was used by a Chinese
businessman who pretended to represent rich Chinese.
Hiding behind our contact in order to escape detection, he
planned to appropriate the Chinese wealth for himself but
to go nowhere. The escapees — including myself and
some members of my family — were abandoned in the
jungle and were arrested, because the plan was leaked. The

Chinese again had to soothe the police with gold before their family members were released from prison.

One afternoon in late 1979, another aimless day without hope, I was talking to Tram, one of my sisters, who had just come to our home from the province. Tram was trying to work out the possibility of how to make ends meet. She was good at sewing and making artificial flowers. Our conversation, however, gradually led to the confusing subject of how to adapt as Christians to live in this difficult situation. I said to Tram, 'I've decided to make myself very clear in my prayers. If soon I have an indication of an acceptable life here, I will not make plans to leave this place any more.'

Tram and I were very close and very helpful to each other. 'Perhaps your help to me in the sewing shop would be the answer for you — or you can help in making flowers.' She went on, 'I think you've been disturbed by the pastor's question. I still want to leave and I'm praying for that chance. I feel it's impossible to live in this situation. Like a fish out of water, the more it struggles the more it gets stuck in the sand.'

I did not know how to answer Tram. I had thought seriously about what I heard from the pastor. I knew he meant it depended on me where I would make the 'green pasture', where I would be content. It could be in my heart, not necessarily in another country.

My gloomy, depressed attitude had recently become more positive. 'I'll ask for God's help. I'll challenge him to reveal his existence to me in a practical way.' Conviction grew in me so that it was as strong as it was during the heartbreaking moments when I was tearfully sitting beside my wounded brother.

Nevertheless, I did not want to show my religious side too much to my sister. I expressed my thought in a different way. 'At least we have the experience of knowing what communism is like.'

'What? What's the use of these ugly experiences?' In a bitter voice, my sister staring at me said, 'I definitely don't need this kind of experience! There's nothing wrong about wishing to live in "green pastures" over there. Actually I disagreed with the pastor for bringing this issue into his sermon.'

I believe Tram did not realise how deeply I struggled between my apparent unwillingness to plan a further escape and my deep wish to leave. I said to her gently, 'It's his spiritual responsibility anyway. I guess I can understand how the shepherds could not help feeling the pain of seeing the drought dry out all the green grass, and the sheep having to move away.'

Tram suddenly stopped talking and went to the front door. A boy of about thirteen or fourteen years of age appeared on his bicycle out the front of my house. He wore a short-sleeved white shirt and a pair of blue shorts. He looked no different from any schoolboy.

'Is this Nam Phuong's home?' I heard the boy ask. He sounded sharp and short. Then came a silence. I was actually in the second room of my house, sitting behind a large cane bookshelf that also acted as a divider between the first and second room. Nobody from outside could see me there. But we were familiar with the house, so we knew where we could see each other through the gaps in the books on the shelf.

I peered through the shelf to the veranda to see what was happening. My eyes suddenly caught my sister's. She blinked at me and shook her head gently. Her expression made me sense instantly that there must be something amiss. She wanted me to stay inside and be quiet.

'Yes, it is. But she's not home at the moment,' I heard

my sister answer the boy.

'When will she be back home?' the boy asked.

'I don't know. She went trading all day. I'll tell her when she comes home,' Tram answered.

'But it must be exactly as it is in the note,' the boy insisted softly but firmly; and he rushed away.

Tram came into the room. She showed me the note — a small piece of paper with a stencilled printed letterhead. It was from the *Van Phong Cong An*, the security police office. The note said, 'You are requested to see the police at the office tomorrow at 9.00 a.m. Reason: *'Cho biet sau'*, 'You will be told later.'

'It's from the *cong an*?' I uttered. I held my breath. Everything whirled before my eyes. My blood seemed to stop running. I was sure my days were numbered!

It was two o'clock in the afternoon. For a moment my sister and I were quiet; but hundreds of urgent considerations crowded our minds.

'Sister, I think you must run away immediately. Otherwise you will be arrested and sent to a labour camp,' Tram suddenly said. She was always the one who made decisions for me.

'But what is the reason — can you guess?' I trembled in confusion. 'I've not yet heard of any former workers of the Americans who've gone to re-education camps.'

Several guesses were made, but they all seemed wrong; until my sister burst out, 'Don't you think it was your meeting with those foreigners in the church? I think that's what it is.'

'Yes, you're right. Painfully right!' These words from my sister came as a complete bombshell. They chilled my blood.

My memory went back some three months. One Sunday morning, instead of going to my regular church, I went to one in the city. I planned to attend the church service and afterwards try to see a relative who was a member of that congregation. My relative had owned a grocery shop for many years. I hoped she would give me an opportunity to earn my own living through her business.

The church was crowded with people. I knew quite a few of them very well. I did not seen my relative, but I thought I would look for her afterwards. While I was walking in, an elderly woman touched my shoulder from behind and whispered, 'Several foreign Christians are coming to church this morning. I heard Belle would be here too.' This was one of the large churches in town where occasionally foreigners came to join the service during their official visits to Vietnam.

I was astounded to hear about Belle, a friend of mine from Australia. 'Why is she here?' I whispered to the lady. 'Should I leave the church right now? This is not what I'd planned to come here for.' I was fully aware of the many 'forbidden acts' in this new society, and meeting with foreigners was one act that was forbidden. While I knew I'd be a fool to meet Belle, in a way it had an attraction for me after years of being forced to shake off my past. I felt hurt and in turmoil within myself when I thought I was even unable to meet my close friends though they were right here.

The friendly lady, who knew of the friendship Belle and I had had, encouraged me. 'I think it's quite normal for people to greet each other at church!' I was tempted by the opportunity; I ignored my worries and stayed.

Belinda — Belle to the Vietnamese — and I had worked for the same organisation in Vietnam for quite a few years during the war. In fact, we were among the very first people to have joined the office. Belle left Vietnam shortly before the communist takeover. Though we had been good friends, I had had no contact with her since then.

When the church service was about to begin, I saw Belle walk in with a European man. They sat down in one of the pews in the front. Later a Vietnamese man came in and sat in the space next to Belle. Had I not been so nervous and looked more closely at the European man — he was in his late thirties — I would have also recognised him as one of the special guests at my former office not long before the war was over. But right now Belle's familiar appearance in her white *ao dai*, the national Vietnamese tunic, and white pants struck me deeply. It was this picture which revived one of the charming fantasies of the past. Yet I realised that past did not exist; otherwise I could have embraced Belle, and cried happily, 'Hello there! What have you been up to for four years? Are you back here for good?' and such warm-heartedness.

'Hi, Phuong!'

'Hi, Belle!'

'Phuong, this is my friend John from Australia. We're here for a special visit to the government.' John was representing a worldwide aid agency.

'Hi, Phuong!'

'Hi, John!'

That was all. These greetings that took place after the church service were trite, but our eyes filled with tears. With the traditional greeting kiss Belle breathed into my ear, 'Sorry, I can't talk to you right now. I think he's a spy.' She gave a quick glance at the man who sat next to her during the service. This brought me back to earth with a thud.

The man who sat next to Belle in the church was actually the driver of the government car assigned to John and Belinda to use around town. Yet he was not only a driver. He became extremely angry when I got in the car because John and Belle invited me to have lunch with them at their hotel. Sensing trouble, I got out of the car and said,

'I won't bother to come with them if it's not all right with you.'

'What's wrong with it?' John said in a raised voice, upset. 'We're friends. Can't she come with us? Can't we have lunch together?'

I was in a totally confused state. Nothing was worse than these moments when I realised how much I was like those mayflies crazily jumping into the killing lights. I wished I had not wanted to see my friends, but it was too late; I had already done it.

'Please get in, Phuong!'

'Sorry, I can't!'

But both John and Belle pulled me into the car.

'Nothing to be scared of, Phuong!' John said in a comforting way. 'We've asked our government host if we can meet our Vietnamese friends if we happen to see them. And his answer was "It's perfectly fine!"'

John and Belle were not used to the laws in the new Vietnam. After being angrily rejected by the security guard at the hotel for taking me — a Vietnamese — into the restaurant located in the hotel where they were staying, John and Belle decided to take me to a restaurant outside.

A man in his thirties walked into the same restaurant shortly after we settled down in our seats. He sat at the opposite table, ordered his food and ate alone. Dark oily skin, long wavy hair shining with brillantine, dark sunglasses, floral printed shirt; this man looked no better than a loiterer. The unattractive appearance of the man, however, stirred our suspicions. We sensed he could be a spy watching us. His lunch lasted as long as ours. Our food became tasteless. In my confusion, my friends' conversation did not make sense to me.

'Please leave me, my friends. I'm extremely sorry — but it's too dangerous for me,' I whispered to John and

Belle when we went out of the restaurant. I slowly walked away from them after the tight handshakes and the unspoken goodbyes.

'*Do-la*? Did they give you any dollars?'

'Oh my God!' I ground my teeth. This was like being on death row. 'Hey kids! Shut up and go away! You know Americans are forbidden here, don't you?' I almost yelled out those words to the street boys who surrounded me when I stood waiting for a cyclo. But I did not. These boys might be the 'booby traps' from the suspected spy, I thought. I put on a false smile, and said, 'No, they're not Americans. They're Australians from Australia.'

I took a cyclo to a friend's place who lived in a different direction to my home. I hoped this would make the spy lose his bearings. When I told the friend what had happened to me, she almost pushed me out of her house. 'I'm sorry, Phuong, but you'll cause the police to suspect me too if you stay here. Please understand.'

'But I'm already here. Please let me stay!' I pleaded. I went up to my friend's room on the second floor of her house. I sat stiff on her bed until evening.

'Yes, you're absolutely right about it, Tram!' I had awoken from my recollections and was alert to my present danger. I said to my sister, 'But I don't think running away is the sol-ution.'

A little girl was playing outside my veranda. It was the small daughter of my friends, a young couple, who lived in the same area. An idea came to me. I called the little girl to come inside, and said, 'Auntie's not well. Please call your mama to come over here quickly, my dear!' Immediately the girl went off and her mother rushed into my house. I told my friend — a trusted friend — about my trouble, and asked her to pass it on to our local church minister. I did this because I was concerned that my sister and I would be watched closely from the time we received the special note.

The message I received from our young minister was that he and his wife would fast from that hour and pray for me for the rest of the day. All my sisters and brothers were frightened. In silence they prayed for me. That night I was so restless. I sat by myself in a dark corner of my small room, visualising what I would have to do the next day. I realised from now on I had to face the danger alone. Even my loved ones could do nothing to save me. A conflict of feelings arose in my mind. In fact, I had just shared with my sister about my recent strong commitment to my faith; now things seemed to turn out completely differently from what I had asked for.

I wished my parents were here to help me. Then, without bidding, some words from a story of the past suddenly came into my mind. They were from the Bible, but from what part of the Bible, or when I had heard them, I could not recall: 'The waters of the Jordan river would not have parted if the people of Israel did not actually put their feet into the water.' Did this mean that I had actually to face the police before God would rescue me? Theologically I understood the message; but I felt terribly afraid to accept this challenge. Somehow an exhausted, tumbled sleepiness dragged me down into its depths until dawn.

I woke up early feeling very clear in my mind. I told my sisters and brothers I felt running away was not the solution. So I was going to see the *cong an*.

At 8.30 a.m. I was ready to leave home. My eldest sister thought it was important for my family to know where I would be in case I did not return home. She suggested that my teenage niece take me on her bicycle to the police station. Before we set off, Tram suddenly reminded me, 'Sister, you must take a small towel and a toothbrush to use in case they do not let you come home.' I thought of my silent but earnest prayer early that morning. I said to my sister: 'No, I won't take anything with me. I've prayed that I'm going to see them now, but he'll let me go home after. If I take those things with me, it means I don't totally trust him.'

I left home carrying with me my usual shoulder bag. It had inside the usual things — a small purse with a small amount of money, a handkerchief, a haircomb, a small hand mirror.

The armed security guard was a *bo doi* in his mid-twenties. From the gate he quietly led me into an area which was about half a hectare in size. The entrance to the area was pleasant with green grass and a few old trees giving ample shade. Several brick houses were scattered around what I thought was the main office of the security police.

I was led a little further, behind this pleasant area where I was aware of a long heavy barbed wire fence overhead. The guard stopped at a small, narrow gate with heavy rusty barbed wire and unlocked the gate. We walked through it. Behind this gate appeared a large area which was totally different from the front. There were at least three tedious rows of wooden shacks running the length of the thin barbed wire dividers between each. All were locked and silent. I could not help but guess, somewhat frightened, that they were criminals' cells.

Finally, I was led to another row of concrete cubicles. Some had doors open from which men in police uniforms came in and out. This area was totally strange and terrifying to me. Later I came to know that this rear section was the police interrogation section.

The guard took me to the last cubicle at the end of the third row. From a huge bunch of keys in his hand, he picked one, unlocked the door with it, and showed me in. 'Sit down and wait here.' That was all he said. He walked away, leaving the door half-open.

I sat down on a rusty steel folding-chair next to a small wooden table. Opposite was an old wooden chair. An electric fan hung from the ceiling. That was all in this matchbox-like chamber. About ten minutes later the fan began to whirl around stronger and stronger.

The suffocating air of the room and my state of being left alone in silence made me feel totally numb. I tried to predict what kind of interrogation or torture I would have to deal with in the minutes to come, but my mind was absolutely blank.

It seemed a century that I was waiting in this empty cage. The door suddenly swung open and a policeman came in unceremoniously. Perspiration poured steadily down my face and my eyes blurred. The security man in his mid-thirties sat down on the wooden chair and threw a stack of papers and a ballpoint pen on the table. He pushed his chair a little backward and raised his face to me with a fresh cigarette stuck in his lips, while dipping his fingers into his shirt pocket to find matches.

'Do you recognise me, Nam Phuong?' he asked, then lit his cigarette, his other hand around the flame to cover it from the windy air.

'Are you kidding?' I thought as I glanced at the man. 'How do I know you?'.

'No, I don't. I'm sorry,' I answered him seriously.

A nasty fist thumped loudly on the table. 'Liar! You should have known me!' He stared at me furiously.

I looked at him straight, trembling. 'I'm telling you the truth. This is the first time I have met you.'

'No!' he stated firmly. 'It's the second time!'

My mind was swimming. I searched my memory. I wondered if this was a trap leading to something else. I recalled nothing.

'Don't try to ignore it. I was in the restaurant with you and your Australian friends Belle and John.'

As if a fist had struck my face, I sat in the chair paralysed.

For about two hours that morning I was then interrogated. Who were my Australian friends actually? What sort of work had they been really doing? Did I know my former office was a CIA network? Did I know there was a tunnel in the US Embassy building, and how far did the tunnel run? Why did I work for this office for so many years? Why didn't I leave the country during April 1975?

'You must write your life story.'

Life story? *Life* story? The echo of those words filled my ears. 'Ah, that rings a bell,' I thought. 'You must be joking! I wrote it three years ago in eight pages with your cracked smudged ballpoint. You know damn well about it. I could add to it the history of the last four years after being "liberated" —if you'd like me to.' However, I was not the kind of a dare-devil, brave woman to actually speak my thoughts.

The picture of the first escape after being abandoned in the jungle was still vivid to me. I had been arrested with the whole group of escapees, including Tram and my two young nephews. At first Tram and I and another young woman of the same group had been detained separately in a dark cell. At night we had slept on the cold filthy cement floor with huge disgusting rats crawling around looking for food along the foot of the wall. The cell borrowed the light from a street light which reflected a shadow the shape of a coffin against the wall. Our survival diet was shoved through the door in something like a battered dirty cat bowl. Then we were transported to a central prison where Tram and I were put in solitary confinement for eight days.

In this 'no-speaking-allowed cell', I was told to reflect

on my crimes towards the Party and State. No washing was allowed for eight days, though I had been through a swampy jungle and had waded in a muddy river. A plastic bucket was used as the basic toilet facility for four in this 'isolation' cubicle. There was an iron bar which ran across the floor. If one of us was secretly reported as breaking this special cell's laws, that person would be chained to the bar.

'Yes, of course I will write it again for you,' I whispered bitterly to myself. And again, like a kind of absurd daydreamer, I switched my mind back to the days when I was a teenager.

At the end of the day I was allowed to go home, but with a strict warning to tell nobody about what had happened to me, even my family. However, the police did not know how much I longed to share with my family this most terrifying event of my life. I told them everything as soon as I got home.

In the morning of the second day, in the same interrogation room, in front of the same security police, the papers which contained my life story were thrown back at me.

'It's a stack of lies!' the policeman shouted at me. 'Not a bit of it is true!' He demanded, 'Write it again!'

He took back my life story written the day before. And before leaving the room, he stressed, 'Remember this. We already know everything about you. We only want honesty from your side.'

Again I was left alone in the dried cement chamber for the whole day writing my life story again. The fear that I might write something that conflicted with what I had written the day before scared me to death.

I came home again at the end of the day extremely exhausted through fear. I remember one of my brothers looking at me; then he took from his pocket the last money he had for that day and urged his other sister, 'Please prepare the best food for her tonight; otherwise she will collapse.' That night during my sleep I was awakened by a shocking dream that the *cong an* secretly knocked at my door and asked me to follow him.

As ordered, I went back to the police office on the third day. 'Today we're going to work at *nha dan*, the people's home,' the policeman said. 'Do you have a bicycle with you?'

'Yes, I have,' I answered.

I was tense. I did not understand what the police meant by 'working at *nha dan*'. However, I rode my bicycle with a policeman in front and another behind. Both were in ordinary clothes. To an observer it was just another common traffic scene. My heart beat and my head felt faint.

About three-quarters-of-an-hour later, we arrived at a house located in the inner city. It was a typical well-to-do-home. It was full of common domestic luxuries which my family and most southerners used to have before the 'down with the US trademark goods' campaign four years before. I wondered who the house's owners were and how they still owned these forbidden luxuries. What was their relation to the police?

I was asked to sit down on a couch next to an electric fan; this was a nice treat in the hot weather. A cup of refreshing Chinese tea was brought up to the table for me. What did these mean for me? I felt suspicious rather than enjoying it.

'So, how have you been living since you've not got a job?' one policeman asked. 'It must be hard for you,' the other added.

I thought I must be careful in my answer. 'I retail goods taken from the wholesalers for small profits.'

'What kind of goods do you normally sell? And how much profit do you get every day?'

'Fish sauce, soy sauce, or handmade washing detergent from co-op shops. With a good list of orders and hard work on my bicycle [I carried all those things on my bicycle in a basket] I can earn about five dong in all. [A government worker's monthly wage was twenty dong and a bowl of noodles for a simple lunch was two-and-a-half dong.] But I must admit I seldom have regular customers.'

'So it doesn't stretch over the days you earn nothing, does it?' The police sounded understanding. 'How would you like a regular job working for the government with a good salary?'

A hope sparkled in my mind. I thought the police saw my honesty and planned a reconciliation for me by giving me a job that would suit my skills. I said emotionally, 'I'd be very happy to work and do whatever I can.'

'In fact, it's a very easy job.' The police officer smiled at me and lowered his voice. 'You'll watch your local church and report to us. That's all you have to do. You'll get a generous monthly salary.'

It was like being injected with an electric current. 'I'm sorry. You mean I'll work as a *spy*? No, I can't do that,' something spurred me to say. 'I go to church to worship the Lord, not to spy upon it.'

'You should know that peace in our country could not have been achieved by only one person, but by the contributions of the whole people. You can't just sit there and enjoy it and do nothing.' His eyes flashed in anger. 'Suppose that you saw someone hide guns in the back of your church. What would you do about it?'

'I've not seen anyone do that sort of thing in church!'

'Go home and think about it.' It was a great surprise that the official let me go home. 'Remember, your life is in our hands. You must report yourself to the police immediately whenever you're wanted,' he warned.

From the time I pulled my bicycle out of that luxurious

house and rode home, I sensed the touch of a mystery which had melted their iron hearts. I wished the police had also sensed it. I was totally in their hands, like a sparrow in a snare, yet somehow they had freed me.

'Yes, I'm back home as I wished and I've told my family!' That night I had a sound, restful sleep. My rough bed with its worn-out mattress and pillow were turned into a green pasture.

My search for a livelihood, however, was ceaseless. I was still unemployed. I went to Can Tho, a large provincial city in the Mekong delta, to trade. The same goods I had traded did not attract people all the time. A cousin and I planned to buy salted food such as fish, prawns and eggs to take to Saigon to resell. These were not listed among the forbidden products. In the provincial market I happened to meet a woman who recognised me as one who had worked in the provincial hospital years before.

After the shock of being touched unexpectedly from behind in this busy, noisy crowd — in truth I thought I was being followed again — I was pleasantly surprised. I still remembered this lady very well. She was the Australian surgeon Scott Macleish's first case of breast cancer. I would not be surprised if Mr Macleish still has her name written in his surgery protocols of this particular year of his career. I called her respectfully *Ba Chin*, Mrs Nine. 'Nine' was the birth order in the family.

This lady — I guessed she was now in her sixties — invited me to her home for a special meal and to meet her family. Her enthusiasm made me think I should not refuse her invitation. I arrived at her home to find everybody in the family was ready to welcome me to a beautiful lunch. I was seated in the middle of a long table of about eight people; opposite me was this lady.

On either side were two men whom I was introduced to as her brothers. Before we started the meal, there was a traditional moment of welcome. 'I'd like to introduce to you this young lady.' Her smiling eyes focussed on the two men. 'She's a part of my existence today.' She pointed at me and continued, 'Ten years ago she introduced me to the wonderful Australian doctors who saved my life. Otherwise I would not have the chance to see you both!'

'Miss Phuong,' this lady said to me, 'I'd also like to introduce you to my two brothers. They came back from Hanoi after the peace four years ago.'

I was numb. I didn't want to meet these two men. I sensed that my identity was revealed, an almost-prisoner of the communists. The police warning still echoed sharply in my ears: 'Your life is in our hands. . . in our hands!' It was like a suspended sentence.

This lady went on emotionally, 'Brothers, you should understand it's only by Miss Phuong's determination to help and because of the generous, skilful Australian doctors that I was able to welcome you back here. I would have died, wouldn't I, Miss Phuong? As the doctors advised me after the surgery, I had a yearly check for five years. The cancer has completely gone.'

The two men said thanks for having the chance to meet me. They invited me to have more food. They looked pleasant.

Afterwards, I went to the kitchen to thank the rest of the family for a delicious meal and their warm hospitality. The lady suddenly came close to me and whispered, 'Why are you still here, miss? I thought you'd have gone that April. What are you doing for a living these days?'

I said to her cautiously, 'It's not easy, Ba Chin. They've never trusted me. They've never given me a job. That's why I have to do this small trading.'

She was touched to tears. 'I wish I could help you. But I've also been blamed by my brothers for not being supportive of the Viet Cong during the war.' She looked to the front room and softened her voice. 'I'll pray for you. I also ask you for a favour. I'm in debt to the Australian doctors, but can do nothing to repay their kindness. Whenever you leave Vietnam and see them, kindly pass on my deep gratitude to them.'

The chance of seeing the Australian doctors again seemed remote, but I did promise this lady that her wish would certainly be fulfilled whenever I got there.

Some time later Tram and I were one of six groups of escapees hidden in six small trading sampans — we had decided to try again to escape. We gathered and departed at different river points, on different days; then we were supposed to meet the big ship at the Ca Mau River estuary together on day six. Unfortunately, the ship had been caught by the marine security a few days before, but we did not know. We floated hidden on the river near the estuary for six days waiting for the ship. Very often we had to protect ourselves against the river police by hiding in a canal from morning till night.

We were attacked by millions of *muoi Ca Mau*, Ca Mau mosquitoes. Ca Mau is the southernmost part of Vietnam touching the Gulf of Thailand. Its dense jungles and mangrove swamps have a worldwide reputation for producing the most dangerous malarial mosquitoes. The local people say the mosquitoes in this area are as big as a hen! There is a saying that two of them can carry you off and throw you into the swamp easily.

Eventually, we almost ran out of food and fresh water. We decided to find our way home; but we had totally lost our direction. In the dark night our sampan mistakenly hit a huge fishing net spread over one-third of the river. It was the fisherman's living for the next day. In the darkness we had to repay him from the little we had — we didn't want a discontented fisherman leaking our secret.

On day eight at night and in rain, our sampan got stuck on the mud bank. We had to bail the water out constantly, while some of us waded in the mud to drag the sampan out to deeper water. We were fifteen in all — ten adults and five children — including a one-month-old baby and a two-year-old girl. While we were going through this shocking crisis, the two-year-old girl's reaction added to our frightful experience. She was extremely restless, screaming unceasingly all the way. Even the strongest dose of sleeping syrup her father forced her to swallow did not quieten her. When we passed the checkpoint, her father had to shut her screaming up by clamping his hand over her mouth, but her small body convulsed like an angry wild cat.

Finally, we ran out of everything. Most of the adults in our sampan took the risk of making their way home on the passenger boat which passed by early that morning. Tram and I were left in the sampan with a young woman and her two boys, and a young man. We had no money left for the boat fare.

It was still early — about 6.00 a.m. We were in a state of total surrender. We did not know where we actually were. In fact, I had never travelled this far in my life. The young man, Nam, was the head of our group. He was a city person who had only learnt how to run a boat in the previous few months. He was using only a hand-drawn map of the river area, but the stormy rain the previous night had washed away everything on the map.

A boat full of green watercress quietly glided along the water. Suddenly it stopped in front of us.

'*E, bi bo ha*?', 'Hey, are you abandoned?' a middle-aged stranger said, lowering his voice.

'Yes! Abandoned!' Nam dropped his voice, depressed. He just did not care any more. He thought sooner or later we would be caught. That short phrase explained everything itself. This stranger undoubtedly knew who we were. We were already in his hands, whether the hands were good or bad. Strangely, the man did not appear to us a bad person.

'Need some help?' he whispered.

'Yes, definitely!' Nam was buoyed up by the sudden offer. 'Petrol! We have run out of petrol! By the way, where are we?' Nam added.

'If you travel this way for about an hour-and-a-half you'll be on the outskirts of Bac Lieu,' the man answered while quickly handing two small plastic containers of petrol to Nam. 'This should be enough to get there,' he said.

Tram then appeared. 'Please help us with some money for bus fares,' she pleaded, though feeling terribly embarrassed. 'Please tell us your address and we'll repay you later.'

Immediately a handful of money was thrown into the sampan. The man started his boat. 'Be quick, otherwise you'll get caught soon.'

The mysterious man sailed his boat away. 'Don't worry about repaying now. We may end up meeting each other again.' An hour-and-a-half later, we shared the money at a small village market on the river bank. It was just enough for the bus fares from the countryside to the provincial city, but it was still a long way to our own provinces.

Nam disappeared immediately as he had worked out his own way. As a young man, it would be a disaster if he was arrested. We, the three women and two young boys, walked to the bus station through the market. After nine days on water, I felt like I was walking on a cloud and my feet did not touch the ground. I almost fell over.

We caught the packed bus, the only one of the day to town, trying to make ourselves inconspicuous. But Yen, the young woman, could only find room on the bus step. All the time I had a frightful feeling of being followed by the police. We arrived at the main town of Bac Lieu. It was about noon and we had run out of money again. We had to walk through the central market, hoping to find help from Yen's relative whom she had not seen for many years. The awful thing was our odd appearance made us stand out in the street: muddy clothes, bare feet and lost frightened looks.

'My God, how miserable you are! Did you try to *vuot bien*? Be quick! Come inside!' Yen's relative led us straight to the back room of her house. 'Where's your husband, Yen? Is he still *hoc tap*, being educated?' the relative asked Yen.

'I've heard nothing from him since he left me for re-education camp. Rumour has it that he might have died somewhere up north.' Yen's husband was a former military major.

There was no time for any kind of emotion. It was necessary to hurry before the security problem affected this family because of our suspicious presence in that home. The kindness from this lady and her husband was unforgettable. We all had showers and we changed into her clean used clothes and sandals which were chosen to fit each of us. She prepared a quick lunch for us. Then she gave us enough money for bus fares for a long trip back to our own provinces and urged us to leave immediately.

On the bus we were all extremely exhausted, not having had proper sleep for nine days. But the anxiety of getting back home as soon as possible kept us awake. Suddenly our bus stopped. I looked out. Another bus had also

stopped ahead of ours. From there I saw the family who
had the screaming child being dragged out by the police.
Tram and I were terrified. The driver of our bus, however,
jumped out and ran up to the police. His attitude looked
funny, but we understood by his manner that he was
asking a favour of the policeman. Immediately, the
policeman waved our bus through.

My parents were startled to see us back home. After
nine days, they thought we would have reached one of the
promised land's asylums, be in gaol or be dead. For three
days all Tram and I did at my parents' home was to sleep,
then wake up and eat, then sleep again.

My parents' home was a two-storey brick house
provided by the church. Though the house was not a new
house, it was attractive and convenient. Our family occupied the second floor which had all the facilities for an
average family. The ground floor was used as my father's
office and guest area. But the ground floor was occupied
by the local authorities. It became too costly as well as
inconvenient to have all the family activities upstairs.

My father built a small thatched hut behind the house.
Under this roof we cooked by using firewood instead of
electricity. Everywhere electricity was cut off every second
day. We washed by using water taken from the river
behind our home instead of tap water, and even had our
evening meals early to keep the electricity bills low. Our
family home on the second floor was now only for resting
and sleeping. After dinner, we sat in the dim light of a tiny
kerosene lamp chatting until bedtime.

After dinner on the fourth day after our return home
from the escape attempt, we were gathering in our living
room as usual, except for my father who tried to work at
the small desk in his bedroom. Suddenly, we heard the
raucous barks of dogs from downstairs and the sounds of

feet on our staircase. Being sensitive to our situation, Tram and I immediately hid in one of our bedrooms.

'Hi, family!' A local young man — in plain clothes and carrying a gun — appeared at our door.

'Hi, what can I do for you?' Van, my young married sister — whose husband was also in the re-education camp and who lived with my parents permanently in this home — answered the door.

'*Chao chi*', 'Hello sister!' the man said, trying to be friendly. He was actually one of the local people. 'Are you having some visitors?'

It was a clear alert to us all. Tram and I did not have a permit to stay at this place. Someone must have seen us while we went down to our kitchen hut to eat with the family. Van immediately answered, 'Yes, it's my relatives.' Van pretended to be normal. 'They always stop here to say hello before going to the camp to visit their husbands each month. But they just left after lunch to catch the bus.'

The man looked around our room suspecting something. A male voice shouted from the yard calling him for something urgent. He quickly left us. That night none of us slept a wink. Tram and I could hardly wait until dawn so that we could go back to Saigon.

Later that evening, my parents had a small quarrel. 'Phuong and Tram must go back to the city immediately, early this morning, before the police check again. I cannot tell lies even to protect my children!' my father said to my mother. He was caught between reality and his desire to be honest and truthful in any situation.

But my mother became angry. 'It's ridiculous!' my mother said, trembling. 'I want them to stay. This is their parents' home. Can't they stay as long as they want?'

Nevertheless, Tram and I left the province very early that morning.

12

Homelessness: 1981 – 1987

I WALKED THROUGH THE BUSTLING PROVINCIAL MARKET which ran alongside the broad Mekong River, with Tuyet and her young son, to meet 'the woman in black'. It was my seventh attempt to flee from my country. It was an unforgettable day in September 1981.

We were not actually supposed to meet this woman, but to watch for her and follow her. We were told she would appear as an attractive businesswoman wearing a fine fabric outfit — a Chinese-style traditional short tunic and a pair of pants. All in black, and black-scalloped embroidered edges. She would carry by her side a large basket for shopping and walk past all the secret waiting spots around the marketplace, while pretending to buy food to fill the pannier. Then she would walk down to the wharf to a passenger ship at the dock. While all this was going on, she would be recognised by the escapees from their secret waiting spots. They would then follow her to the passenger ship.

This provincial market was the secret gathering point where the organiser — the woman in black — was to collect a small proportion of the escapees who were joining her trip. At least fifteen people were secretly involved in this escape effort. None of the escapees was aware of the existence of the others.

It was frightening when you did nothing, but wandered for hours — because the secret contact had not yet shown up — in an unfamiliar busy place for a hidden criminal purpose. But it was more difficult when you had to keep an eye out for the watchful police or suspicious people, at the same time not losing sight of the moving black figure in the tangled crowd of a large bustling market. You certainly appeared as an oddity when you were not 'doing the market in the market', but colliding with countless people, because your eyes were focussed on something else.

I was in a cold sweat. I grabbed my sister's hand and her hand was in her son's. We walked past the wharf to the passenger ship. The woman in black — she was in her early forties — sat down on a long bench against the side of the boat among the passengers. Underneath her seat was her full shopping basket.

She chatted pleasantly with some. She gazed around. Suddenly she stood up. 'My God!' she yelled out to the man who was busy starting the engine. 'I've forgotten to pick up my rice. Would you mind if I run back and get it?'

A raucous outburst of disappointment came from the passengers. Everybody was anxious to get back to their remote villages as soon as possible after a long morning of doing their routine market, perhaps for the whole month. The woman rushed back to the market for about ten minutes, then returned with a heavy bag of rice. Behind her were a few more passengers. 'You see!' she told the boat man, 'you'd have missed some more profit if you hadn't waited for me!'

In truth, the woman's 'run-back' was just her last 'catch' of escapees.

Amidst the ceaseless chattering among the passengers

and the monotonous sounds of the ship's engine, my memories flooded back a long way to the six years of hardships that our family had borne and my six escape attempts. Most of the attempts I had tried were with my sister Tram. My feelings were in turmoil at that moment.

Would I make it this time? Would I get caught and be put in gaol like I was the first time? Was I right to leave this time when I had already committed myself to be wherever God wanted me to be? Why did the organiser agree for our 'fare' to be paid afterwards? Why was she so kind to me and my nephew? Why was Tram not with me this time? Most of all, had I been pulling their leg about going? The fact that I had left home so many times for this purpose, only to come back, made my sisters and brothers disbelieve me.

It seemed only a moment before that I had left home early in the morning for this escape attempt. The previous night I had said goodbye with little emotion to my brothers and sisters. Anh made a joke about his doubts for this trip. 'Are you joking? I bet I'll see you again in the next few days.'

Ly whispered emotionally, 'Godspeed!' He borrowed the words 'Godspeed' from an English song. It seemed that speaking in another language was the best way to wish me success and at the same time, in a strange way, to disguise his doubt.

'But if you do die at sea,' Anh said, 'I'll try to worship your wandering soul by having a black coffee every day.' Anh joked about me being a coffee lover, even though I could not now afford it. This was not a real joke — it was a cry from a bitter heart. Living or dying in this situation were the same. Perhaps dying at sea was the perfect liberation.

Even so, in the quietness of the early morning, my sister

Tram opened the door for me cautiously, her eyes welling up with tears. 'Please make it this time, dear sister,' she whispered. 'I don't wish to see you again!'

It was indeed an absurd feeling. It was half-moving and half-funny. Like many other times, I did not know whether I would make it or not this time. If I did not, my last words to my family would become laughable. 'Sorry, Tram, that we can't make it together this time!'

The trip was organised mostly for the organiser's family members and close friends. Later some were added in as 'passengers without payment in advance'. This special favour was only for those who had relations with foreigners in the past. Tram had missed out because of this condition.

'Don't worry, sister! I pray I'll find another opportunity soon.'

Tram was always very positive and confident in whatever she was doing. At home she was like my manager with her charm and determination. She would drag me out of bed on Sunday to go to church when I felt I liked my cosy bed better. Or she would decide when it was time for a visit to our parents, and what to buy as gifts to take home for them. She was very helpful and supportive of everybody. I felt myself very much attached to her.

Her words helped me feel hopeful that she would make her way out of Vietnam soon after me.

On that darkest September night in 1981, we negotiated the winding canals to the angry stormy sea. There was a strong mixture of fear, danger and uncertainty in all of us.

When I emerged from the hold of the boat in which seventy-one people — including twenty-five children — were packed, everything had been transformed to a wonderful white morning. Even the woman in black was no more in black. She had changed to something 'real'.

Yes, her real name was Bach Tuyet, meaning 'white snow', the same name as my eldest sister.

'We've passed out of Vietnamese territorial waters. We're safe now,' Tuyet told me.

As I looked over the vast ocean, my mind went back over all the things that had happened during this escape effort. After being on the passenger ship for three hours and jammed in with hundreds of passengers plus luggage and all sorts of things, we had suddenly turned into a narrow canal with heavy vegetation on each side, and had stopped. It was already late in the afternoon. Tuyet raised her voice to the pilot. 'Is the boat going to give us a hard time?'

'Unfortunately, it is. It'll take a while to fix it. It's quicker if you or whoever want to get off here and take local transport to the village,' the boatman answered.

Tuyet did not waste a minute. She dropped the shopping basket into the water, then jumped! There was no time to think. We were asked to watch and do exactly what she did. We all jumped into the muddy water — my sister Tuyet, Khoa, myself and about another fifteen people. We stared at each other bewildered. A beautiful young woman had sat quietly next to me all the way to here, but we did not give each other a hint that we would be in the same boat.

In silence we waded through the mud, following the woman in black to the dark raffia house set in lush green surroundings. It was now about four o'clock in the afternoon.

'You should not come all the way to here!' Tuyet said to my sister. 'You must leave right away. This house will be searched soon after we leave tonight.'

'I only want to say goodbye and thank you, Chi Tuyet, from the bottom of my heart. I'll treasure your kindness!' my sister said through her tears.

'Don't worry too much! Perhaps Buddha will help me get through this time because I've been helping people!' Tuyet told my sister. 'You must hurry and leave this place, otherwise you'll get caught.'

My sister hurriedly kissed me and Khoa, her son. 'Goodbye, you two! Take care of yourself and take care of Khoa for me, Phuong. I must go now.'

Floods of tears signalled my sister's departure. A part of my own self had left me as I painfully watched my sister walk out of our hiding place. 'When do I see you again, sister?' I whispered.

On the way back home on the unfamiliar road of the Mekong delta, my eldest sister became totally lost, fearful and insecure, until at last she saw the sign of a church. It was another crisis and story added to her life which had been tattered since the peace had come.

It was about 8.00 p.m. Thick darkness transformed the whole area, obscuring the raffia-roofed house. A weird silence overtook the fifteen strangers, packed into the tiny dark space. Suddenly a low, firm male voice whispered, 'Listen, everybody. Time to leave. Follow the light of the torch and make no noise at all. Got it?'

The light flashed on and off and we were led to the escape boat.

As my small nephew and I sat in the darkness of the hold of this boat, trembling with silent fear, the voice of a girlfriend came back clearly: 'You must take the pill regularly if you plan to escape. This is what I've been doing for myself in order to survive unharmed from attacks by the *cuop Thai Lan*, the Thai pirates'. The Thai pirates had appeared on the boat people's escape routes to the international refugee asylums set up in Thailand, Malaysia, Indonesia and Singapore. They beat and robbed the refugees until they were naked and dead. All the women on a boat were attacked and raped savagely in front of their helpless husbands, fathers and brothers.

Other people who were concerned about the pirates even suggested that the women must avoid being raped by spreading over their faces and bodies the traditional *mam nem*, the mud fish — nobody could bear its revolting smell.

I also thought of a small group of young people from one extended family whom I knew very well. They contributed their gifts of singing and playing music to the church. This group left the city and were forever lost in the mysterious ocean.

I also remember a man who lived in my suburb in Saigon fleeing the country in a little boat. His boat was caught and dragged back by the marine security when it had almost passed outside Vietnam's territorial waters. The man was in great despair. He whispered to his friend in the same boat, 'I've told my family I want either freedom or death.' He jumped into the water. His body was found a few days later. The police found his identity and, instead of sending his body home to the family, they put it on display in his local community hall for people to view, a case of a country's traitor.

Many such tragedies have happened to people unexpectedly and violently on the way to seek freedom; however, this does not seem to have stopped people from leaving. Clearly, freedom has been sought at all costs, even the cost of life.

We were packed together like sardines along with a lot of coconuts in the hold of the boat. On the floor were lengths of rough timber for sitting. There was so little light that we could hardly recognise each other, even though it was daytime. Above us was another level and another group of people. The deck was for the crew where there was a huge pile of fresh coconuts.

On our second day at sea, at about 3.00 p.m., a strong wind blew up and the boat rolled in the huge waves. A large sombre cloud emerged and within a minute our tiny boat was drenched in pouring rain. Lightning and thunder were unceasing.

We escapees were terrified. Though we had not met pirates and were still in good health, we knew deep down we would not survive much longer in this storm if some miracle did not take place. The 'navigator', a middle-aged schoolteacher, knew very little about the sea and admitted that our boat had lost its way. The boat was like a little leaf crazily dragged around and around in an immense whirlpool. I overheard that there was no safety equipment on board.

In the dim light I saw my nephew sitting against the side of the boat, his head rolling from side to side. He was terribly seasick. He murmured hopelessly, 'Auntie, can I have a bit of lemon?' I felt I needed it too, but there was none. We were told not to bring anything with us to avoid police suspicion. Moreover, we believed we would be provided with basic food and drink during the journey. I did not answer my nephew. I felt so sick in body and mind.

Someone kicked me hard in the stomach. There was a horrified scream from next to me — someone vomited in the other's face! A disgusting, nauseous smell spread all over the place. 'Can I have a bit of water, please?' I murmured. I felt terribly thirsty. I knew people outside were collecting rainwater to drink. We had plenty of fresh coconuts in the boat; but at that stage we wanted to save them until a more desperate need. Nobody responded to what I had asked. 'Water, please!' I said, raising my voice.

From a corner a man shouted, 'Can someone outside hear us? We need water!' After that a small bucket of rainwater was passed around; but when it came to me —

the one who actually asked for it — there was nothing left.

I prayed hard. I knew I would be the first to die. I could not endure this hardship any longer.

At about 5.00 p.m. the storm seemed to ease up a little. Through the thick veil of rain, unmistakable signs of shipping appeared.

'Here they are!'

'The ships! The rescuers!'

Cheers burst from those on the boat. 'Come on, people! Shout and signal!' the navigator urged everyone. The boat kept crashing against the towering angry waves.

'Help! Help!'

I heard them calling, but from my position in the hold I did not know what they were actually doing to stop those ships. Their voices were lost against the mighty waves. The large commercial ships gradually disappeared.

It was about 6.00 p.m. The wind had gone, the storm had eased up and the sea was less rough. But the rain was still pouring down. There was total darkness. Everybody was quiet. When would there be another chance?

'Is it another ship?' a man shouted.

The boat shook. Inside everyone sprang up as if they had just been transfused with new blood.

'Yes, it is! It's coming!'

'It's a ship!'

The outline of a ship broke through the curtain of rain and gradually moved towards our boat.

'Everybody! At all costs we have to stop this one!' the navigator yelled down the hold.

At his urging, we drew from our carrying bags clothes, towels, underwear — our luggage for the journey — and gave them to him to use as fuel. Buckets of diesel were quickly transferred from the hold to outside for soaking the clothing. Within a minute a beacon of fire was held up as our signal.

'Help! Help!' all the men outside shouted out and waved. Suddenly a violent gust of wind swept across, breaking the lighted stick. Everything sank back into darkness and silence.

'Don't worry, people! They're coming!' one of the men shouted from outside. 'Try to make as much noise as possible so they can hear us!'

Inside we started to bang our hands against all sorts of things close to us.

The large ship could now be seen clearly, but was still not very close to us. We heard the engine of a small motorboat coming towards us. Then a brilliant cluster of light from a torch suddenly broke through the darkness onto our boat.

'Oh no! The Thai pirates!' a woman screamed in panic.

'Shut up, woman!' one of our men yelled into the hold. 'They're Indians!'

'Beware of people who will drag us back home! We must fight against it!' a young man said. He sat right in a corner; he could hardly see anything.

'Hands up!' A tall dark naval officer shouted out from his motorboat. Nobody could clearly pick up what this man had said at first. My nephew, in a state of concern for all, called to me, 'Auntie, try to come out to help. I think he speaks English!'

'No! We're not sure yet! They may be pirates!' I said. We all sat quietly awaiting our fate.

The naval officer still stood in his small boat with several others in a cautious watching manner and shouted out again, 'Hands up! All of you!' The navigator translated and we all did as he said. The torch swept around the boat, searching every corner. Then they turned back to their ship after telling our men, 'Stay where you are. We're going to help you!'

No words can convey the feelings of the refugees during these moments of being so close to death. Later we realised that the ship rescuing us was also cautious about being attacked by pirates. The lights of the large ship shed a beam of light that covered a huge area. From our tiny boat I looked up at the giant shape and the lofty height of the ship. I thought I might not survive being rescued!

The actual rescue took place from about 6.00 p.m. to 9.00 p.m. amidst heavy squalls and angry waves. The procedure was that a long rope ladder was to be dropped from the deck to our boat and was balanced and secured by the ship's crew from the deck. When our turn came — one by one — we were to grab hold of the ladder and climb up to the deck.

'Listen, everybody!' shouted a member of the crew from the deck. 'Women first! Can everybody hear? Women first!'

We were all drenched, dishevelled and trembling on the rocking boat as we watched for the chance for each one. The boat, as tiny as a leaf, was swung away by a mountainous wave, then dragged back sharply against the ship. The first woman to climb jumped forward, caught the swinging ladder and held on tightly, gripping the rung of the ladder.

'Excellent! Keep going, keep going!' came the shout from the deck.

The woman sank against the swinging rope, startled. She could not make her body move upward. 'Come on! Push yourself up! Step up!'

Everybody held their breath. We thought if it worked it could only be a matter of luck, not our skill. Finally, the first woman reached the top of the ladder and was hauled onto the ship.

'I'll try! And then you, Phuong!' Chau, who belonged

to the 'missing-at-sea family', said. 'We must be quick! Our boat might soon break up!'

I felt like I was being hanged on death row. I thought I could never make it.

As soon as Chau spoke to me, the ladder was dropped down for the next one. Chau reached for the swinging ladder. She caught it. But while her feet were at the same time supposed to cling to the rung, they missed it. Chau hung loosely against the ship wall above the black ocean. 'Hang onto the rope tightly!' the captain shouted from the deck.

'Don't panic! We're helping you!' another crew member yelled out.

The scene gave me the shivers! What would I do if she actually dropped into that black water? She was my friend. Hanging onto the swinging ladder by her hands, Chau turned backward, her eyes wide and white, her teeth biting into her lip. The flooding rain, wild wind and tempestuous sea continued their fury. All of a sudden a strong gust of wind swept the boat back against the ship again. Miraculously, that was the moment Chau let go of the rope and dropped back onto our boat. Did the angel of death in a whimsical moment change her mind unexpectedly?

Because of what happened to Chau, the captain had a better idea. An extra rope was lowered. We tied the rope around our chests. We still had to help ourselves get on the ladder, but we were secured by being tied and pulled up by the crew at the same time.

My nephew, a capable little boy, was already on the deck when I got there. All the children, in fact, were transferred to the ship in a basket by crew members.

Exhausted and weakened, we stood on the deck watching our little boat gradually sink. The coconuts floated up and down on the high waves together with pieces of the broken boat.

On that dark evening of 19 September 1981, 1 400 kilometres from Singapore, on the way to Pakistan — the commercial vessel's country of origin — a decision was made and seventy-one souls were saved. That decision was made by the captain and the crew of the *Al Hasan* of Pakistan. We were the first refugees, one of the officers told me, to be rescued by that vessel. On previous trips, they had to by-pass refugees because they had not been commissioned by the United Nations to become the 'boat people's angel' at sea.

We spent three days and three nights on the ship in the care of the captain and his crew. They had to change their schedule to take us to Singapore.

It was the first time I had met Pakistanis. One of the young officers told me how he had seen our bobbing boat through the storm — he was on duty that night — and how he reported to the captain every movement of our boat. It was a moving account for the boat people.

I shall treasure the angelic *Al Hasan* in my heart for the rest of my life. It is a unique memorial to human love and compassion.

*   *   *

When the tall, middle-aged Australian man with dark sunglasses and thick beard appeared in front of my hostel room and asked me in my own language, '*Co nhan ra toi khong?*', 'Do you recognise me, miss?' it sent shivers down my spine.

'Oh no! Are you still after me?' I thought. 'I'm so sorry, but I don't remember you.' Again it sounded exactly the same as if I was still in that investigation room! 'No, I'm not there at the moment,' I assured myself. 'I'm in Australia for sure!'

The man took off his dark sunglasses. He burst into amused laughter. His big smile suddenly, unexpectedly brought back memories.

'You're Mr Keo from Vietnam, aren't you?' I stared at him and asked.

'That's right!' he said, nodding his head, his voice sounding absolutely familiar. 'Mr Keo and Mr Le! It's the same me!' His real name was Stuart Bradley. We shook hands excitedly. 'Goodness me! Your thick beard and dark sunglasses make you totally different!' I laughed, astounded at the unexpected meeting. 'How did you know I was here?'

Another man suddenly jumped out from his hiding spot outside my hostel room. It was one of the pastors who looked after Vietnamese refugees in Melbourne. 'From this old man!' Stuart joked. 'But he hid himself just to tease you!' We all laughed happily.

Stuart was an Australian soldier serving in Vietnam during the war and had been a good friend to me in Saigon. When he was off duty, he used his time to the best effect by doing volunteer work to help poor children and orphans in the orphanage in whatever way appeared worthwhile. It was through this charity work that my friends and I came to know him.

He spoke Vietnamese fluently. He chose to be called by a Vietnamese name — Mr Le, meaning 'propriety', one of the five cardinal principles of Confucian ethics. But close Vietnamese friends gave him the nickname Mr Keo, meaning 'Mr Lolly'. It was because lollies were the snacks he normally gave us for fun when we worked together. Lollies are sweet and seemed appropriate because it's how we thought of him. Le became a church minister after his Vietnam days and has been involved in a lot of work to help Vietnamese refugees.

After that, Le contacted a Christian organisation in order to find a job for me. 'Can you recall the name of any Australian friends who are living and working in

Melbourne?' Le asked me.

'I'm sorry, it's such a long time ago. I don't think the people will be the same.' But after Le's phone call and an invitation to visit the organisation, what a coincidence it was when I shook hands with John Rogers at his office. It was John whom I had met with Belinda at the church in Vietnam two years before. Three months later through John's kind help I was given a clerical job in the organisation where he had been working.

*   *   *

My nephew and I finally settled in the new country. I had a permanent job, a small place to live in, a renewed confidence in life and my nephew was enrolled in school.

I would never have believed that sixteen years after our farewell, most of the Australians whom I had met and worked for in Vietnam would still hold our friendship dear. A number of my old friends were still living in Melbourne and were thrilled to see me again.

One day during a brief visit to Scott Macleish's hospital office, I was shown his surgery protocol book of the year when he worked in my provincial hospital. This reminded me about the lady with breast cancer. In passing on her special thanks to Scott, I became conscious of how amazing it was that I was now in Australia and it was possible to keep my impossible promise to this lady.

Mine was now a wonderful feeling of living in real freedom, of being totally independent in mind and heart, of finding the possible in many things which were considered impossible under the oppressive Vietnamese regime. But the most beautiful feeling of all was being respected and trusted as a normal human being. The nightmares of my past were being transformed into hope and encouragement. I enjoyed so much about this new country — blooming spring, the longest days of summer, golden autumns and bracing winters — but it was the peaceful way of life that attracted me the most, a complete contrast to my war-torn country.

However, it is true that 'Home is where your heart is' — I was a woman with a divided heart! The stronger my love for my adopted land was, the deeper I missed my homeland. I was like a lonely goldfish living in a bowl, missing the real moss and weeds. Until, that is, I visited Vietnam again.

Tan Son Nhat Airport at Ho Chi Minh City (formerly Saigon city) looked so tiny and quiet with its handful of people. It was hard to believe it had once been one of the busiest airports in the world.

'Here is my homeland! Here are my people!' As my feet touched the soil, my heart searched for a warm feeling for the land of my birth. Instead, I felt a coldness and indifference. Suddenly all the troubles of the past, the anxiety of being an untrusted person flooded back into my mind vividly.

'Nam Phuong!'

'Yes!'

I moved forward to the counter to present myself at the immigration checkpoint. The Vietnamese official looked at my passport, then gave me a cold look as if he meant to say, 'You're kidding! You're Vietnamese from head to toe and you say you're Australian!' My hands trembled and my knees knocked. I thought how silly I was to bring myself back to this complicated life, to exchange the freedom I had found for this suffocating feeling.

In early 1987, Vietnam started to promote a new policy, *doi moi*, economic reform — an 'Open Door' policy to set up communication with the West. The policy aims to improve the country's economy which has gone downhill since the takeover in 1975.

The policy includes such important areas as foreign investment, joint venture business and tourism. Foreigners are invited to visit Vietnam as tourists. Former Vietnamese refugees who now live around the world are also welcome to come home as tourists.

Despite this new apparent openness, all my friends felt apprehensive when I talked about my idea of returning to visit my family. And so did I! Nevertheless, this idea impelled me after I heard that my elderly father had had a severe stroke. I knew time for my parents was short. It had to be now or it would be too late. And so I went back. It took all my nerve to make the decision.

In the airport waiting area, on the other side of the barrier, were the dear faces of my family. 'Hello there! I won't be long!' I waved to them excitedly. Within a moment all the regrets melted.

As soon as I left the airport, I had a strange feeling. Things were not the same any more. The busy, warm life of a hospitable people had completely gone. Instead, everywhere I went there was coldness, suspicion and apprehension.

In the hotel I started to fill out the security form given to the 'artificial foreigners', the former Vietnamese citizens, to fill in. 'When and why did you leave Vietnam?' I stared at those questions on the form. Perspiration poured down my face and my eyes blurred. Then I was advised that if I wished to go out of the city I must obtain a travel permit; otherwise my own security was not guaranteed.

During my stay at the hotel, I saw among the staff a young woman who resembled an old friend of mine. I thought it must be my friend's sister. Several times I wanted to talk to her for friendship's sake. But the young woman gave no chance for a friendly approach. This saddened me — it was obvious that the situation in my country has changed and my people also had changed, though at heart we are a friendly people.

On the street, some empty taxis and pedicabs were parked around waiting wearily for foreigners and Vietnamese tourists. Several cyclo drivers stormed me and invited me to take a cyclo. However, when I sat on the rusty vehicle, the driver described the hardships of their life, but I was determined to keep my mouth shut. Though my heart cried out for him, I was more concerned for my own safety. In this society, 'spying and suspicion' is the method of controlling people. Anyone could be the object of suspicion by the secret police.

Another time I went in a taxi; I could not help wondering how this driver — a frail man — could make his antique Renault move. This man told me he would take me back to the hotel if I told him the time. I refused, concerned it would cost me a lot to keep a taxi for many hours. But the man laughed — there was a sense of bitterness in his laugh — 'You still think life is like it was before 1975? I might hang around the hotel for two days and make no trips at all! I'll take you back anyway.' It was a twenty-five-kilometre trip and he charged me fifteen thousand dong, about US$2.50. On that day he made five dollars in all from me. He was overwhelmed as if he had found a goldmine. I was told it was about equivalent to the fortnightly wage of a trained doctor in Vietnam today.

One morning I walked along Nguyen Hue Street. A poor woman was sitting between the two baskets of ripe mangoes she was selling. I passed the woman before I had the idea of buying this delicious fruit. I came back. When I asked her about the price, her bright eyes stared at me. 'Oh! Is it true the Super Power is still working a wonder?'

'What's all that about?' I could not help laughing at the woman's funny attitude.

'I've been sitting here almost all morning and nobody has even looked at my fruit,' she explained to me with captivating charm. 'When I saw you passing me, I was disappointed. I said a quick prayer to the *Ong Dia*, the Earth God, and you came back! It's amazing!' I bought a dozen mangoes from her. The woman said thanks to me, believing that the Super Power was still in control of her situation.

Then another day I went to the coffee shop in the Continental Palace Hotel for a cup of coffee. This hotel used to reflect the Paris lifestyle of the French. Scattered around in the coffee lounge was a handful of European customers sitting and sipping the local coffee, dark and bitter. The city air was oppressive, but from the back of the shop came a beautiful piece of classical music reflecting the golden days of this historic hotel. Every note of music evoked the happy sounds of the past. A middle-aged man with the air of a sophisticated waiter — white suit and black bow tie — came and took my order.

'A cappuccino, please,' I said. The man looked dazed. It was a kind of drink which was not known in this grand-styled coffee lounge.

Through the shopping arcade in the hotel I walked to a lacquerware shop with its traditional south Vietnamese products. There was a European middle-aged couple browsing in the shop. The language they were speaking was not English. I asked the shop assistant, 'What nationality are those people? They're definitely not American or French.'

'No, they're Russian,' the woman answered.

'What most attracts the Russians to buy in your shop?' I asked by way of conversation.

She shrugged her shoulders. 'Nothing. They're penniless. They can only afford the old goods in the Saigon flea market. They're the poorest tourists.'

I continued my stroll of the nearby streets to another
tourist gift shop. As soon as I walked into the shop, a
young woman attendant stared at me bewildered. 'Are
you Nam Phuong, sister?' She cupped her hand over her
mouth and lowered her voice. After a glance, I was shocked to realise that she was the young sister of Chau who
was in the same escape trip with me.

It was 6.00 a.m., the last hour before I checked out of the
hotel to leave Saigon. Breakfast was not quite ready in the
restaurant.

I stood near the window of this top-floor restaurant in
one of the best hotels in town, looking over the city. In the
thick atmosphere of the bittersweet morning was the
familiar stretch of water, the Saigon River. It was the same
river which witnessed the heartbreaking farewell thousands
of people gave their motherland. Through the open window I could inhale the sweet scent of air, the natural early
morning scent of Asia. It is unique and indescribable. To
sense it and be inspired by it, one must be an early bird
and must equip oneself with a romantic instinct. The
overwhelming aroma gives you a sense of melancholy,
loneliness and nostalgia.

From somewhere in my sentimental heart echoed an old
song. In my mind I could see a schoolfriend from my teens
standing on the school stage and singing this song from her
heart one summer evening:

Ve day nhin may nuoc bo vo,
Ve day nhin cay la xac xo,
Ve day dau con phut xum vay,
Dau con tham niem say,
Lanh lung ngam troi may. . .

Noi xua oi gio day nat tan,
Do vang khong nguoi sang,
Thon xom trong dieu tan. . .

Returning home is only to see the heavy clouds
and the lonely stream of water.
Returning home is only to see the bare trees
and the falling leaves.
Home is here, but where are the dear moments of
togetherness? The same dear people of the past?
The warm cherished feelings?
Only the cold air of the sky and earth is left to feel!
Alas! The old dear place now is in tatters,
the river ferry is quiet and the boats are empty.
The villages are in ruins.

I had rediscovered this song which word for word
accurately expressed the pain of my heart about my
homeland and my people — a land that was in tatters and
whose people were hurting, lonely and worn-out.

The impact of seeing my home country, Vietnam, so run
down and the life of the people so hard broke my heart —
especially when I saw the unbelievable transformation of
my family, my friends and my neighbours. They had gone
from something to nothing, retreating from the world, from
life. Most painful of all, I saw that they had lost their hope
in the future.

The family home, formerly full of bliss and enchantment,
was now quiet and cold. My parents were like two
withered leaves hanging on a bare tree, waiting to fall.
Happiness helps people grow old with dignity, but sorrow
makes them like ghosts.

I saw my brothers and sisters. They were like lost birds
in a storm, tired and shabby. One of them was the man

who had paid seven years of his life in forced labour for being a 'capitalist'. Yet the mental war, the result of his being brainwashed, had had an even more destructive effect on him. Tears were shed the moment I held his hands in mine. His wife — my eldest sister — now is quiet and has retreated. Her hair showed the colour of passing time. I sat and talked with them on the night that the electricity was cut off. By the dim light of a small candle, I saw that they had no way to mend their broken dreams.

My nephew, a twenty-one-year-old who had returned from the bloody war in Cambodia, had no prospects of a job. I asked him how much he was paid for his risky assignment in another war-torn corner of the world. His answer was 4 000 dong per month — about eighty cents, the price of a can of Coke!

The authorities have now appealed to the outside world for a helping hand to assist the country, a country in ruins with people hurting. It is all the costly result of pride and hatred. There is no payment sufficient to make up for the material and mental damage done to the country. Time that is gone, like a running river, cannot return. Only sincere repentance on the part of Vietnam and generous offers from the world can help.

On a Sunday during my visit I went to the local church. A destitute, shabby individual in the congregation was invited to stand up to say the blessing for the whole church. It was a congregation member recently released from re-education brainwashing camps — after fifteen years! He was one of the million people who fled from north to south during the 1954 exodus.

From his seat at the front he turned to face the congregation, raised his skinny arms straight up and said, 'But now abides faith, hope, love, these three; but the greatest of these is love. Amen!' There was a strong sense of God's presence after those words from one who had survived the valley of death. Indeed, his words demonstrated that 'love does not take into account a wrong suffered'.

It was only in this moment that I realised who I really was. Here were two conflicting philosophies of life — Marxist and Christian — and I surely knew where I stood. But I also saw, in this worn-out remnant of humanity, the only way evil could be defeated, by love triumphing over hatred and faith over fear.

Breakfast was now ready and we all sat down. I could see about two-thirds of the tables in the restaurant occupied by the Vietnamese 'tourists' who had just finished their visit to their families.

The set breakfast menu in this fine restaurant was very basic — bread and butter and jam for European people and pork buns and rice porridge with salted duck eggs or with traditional gherkins — cucumbers soaked in fish sauce — as a choice for Asian tourists. Everything had to be paid for in dollars, not because of the quality of the food, but because of the special taste of poverty. The unbelievable destitution of my homeland!

Suddenly a bat — a really large one — lurched from a neglected corner of the restaurant across the room, back and forth, trying to find a way out.

I had returned to my homeland only to exchange my feelings of nostalgia for the reality of life without love and compassion. My country was like a deserted mother standing shivering in the sombre winter, waiting for the dawn to warm her up.

How much longer will it be before this cold winter is over?

While this book is factual,
some names have been changed to
preserve anonymity.